MASTER YOUR MONEY WITH NUMEROLOGY

Establish Wealth With Numerical Intelligence, Unlock Financial Fortune, Conquer Hidden Obstacles, and Achieve Lasting Prosperity

Sooraj Achar

www.soorajachar.com

YOUR FREE GIFT !!

A s a token of my thanks for taking out time to read my book, I would like to offer you a **Free-Gift**:

Claim Your Free Guide – One Click or Quick Scan Is All It Takes!

Learn 395+ Surprising Psychology Words That Will Change The Way You Think - in the Next 30 Days!

You can also grab your **FREE GIFT** by typing in the below URL: **https://sooraj.soorajachar.com/free-gift**

ABOUT AUTHOR

S ooraj Achar, an Accomplished Author of **35+ Books -** A Sensational **#1 Bestseller Across the Globe**

Dive into the world of **Sooraj Achar**, a prodigious author hailing from Bangalore, India, whose exceptional journey is as intriguing as the profound concepts explored in his works. Sooraj has transcended borders, achieving the coveted status of **#1 Bestseller** in the United States, the United Kingdom, Canada, India, and Australia.

A Remarkable Beginning:

Sooraj Achar's extraordinary odyssey commenced in the vibrant city of Bangalore, India. As a young dreamer, his fascination with mathematics sparked an early connection with the enigmatic world of numbers. This infatuation, initially drawn from captivating numerological stories, sowed the seeds for a lifetime dedicated to the exploration of **Numerical Mysteries**.

A Multifaceted Expert:

Today, **Sooraj Achar** stands as not just an accomplished Software Engineer but also a passionate connoisseur of **numerology** and the ancient science of **Feng-Shui (Vastu)**. His multifaceted persona extends to **coaching and consulting**, where he delves into the profound questions of Health, Relationships, Careers, and Finances. Sooraj is a certified **Ho'oponopono & EFT Healer and NLP Practitioner**, renowned for his transformative abilities in bringing about balance, harmony, and fulfillment in the lives of countless individuals.

A Seeker of Wisdom:

Sooraj's relentless quest for knowledge has led him to the intricate realms of human psychology and behavior. His dedication to understanding the human psyche and optimizing life's potential is unwavering. As a perpetual learner, he embodies the principles of optimal living and shares his wisdom to empower others to lead resourceful lives.

A Believer in Unlimited Potential:

Above all, **Sooraj Achar** is a firm believer in the limitless potential residing within each individual. He ardently champions the idea that every person possesses the capacity to achieve far beyond their self-imposed limits. Through his words and wisdom, he inspires others to unlock their hidden potential and lead lives of purpose and abundance.

For more life-altering insights, delve into Sooraj Achar's remarkable catalog of books. Visit www.soorajachar.com and embark on a journey of self-discovery and transformation.

Stay Connected:

Explore the latest updates, thought-provoking content, and inspiring messages from Sooraj Achar by connecting with him through our social media channels. Join us in the pursuit of a fulfilling and harmonious life.

https://amzn.to/3CgQHF9

https://medium.com/@soorajachar99

https://bit.ly/3M7gIu2

instagram.com/psychology_of_numberz/

https://bit.ly/3dO6aDh

https://bit.ly/3LXBTyz

https://bit.ly/3E9vKxc

ACKNOWLEDGMENT

How does a person say "**Thank You**" when there are so many people to thank?

Obviously, this book is a big thank you to my father **G Sathyanarayan Achar,** who is a powerful role model, and my mother **G Pramila,** who taught me love and kindness.

I extend my heartfelt appreciation to my sister, **Shruthi S**, brother-in-law, **Saravana P**, and adorable niece, **Naveeksha S**, who have played pivotal roles in making this book a reality. Their presence makes my life complete.

A special acknowledgment is reserved for my mentor, **Mr. Arvind Sood**, whose guidance led me to become a **Numerology and Vaastu Coach and Consultant**. I am privileged to have received permission to use the term "Driver-Conductor," a creation of Mr. Arvind Sood.

I owe thanks to **Mr. Som Bathla**, an **Amazon #1 Bestselling** author, for his mentorship, motivation, and guidance in the realms of **Writing, Self-Publishing, and Launching Books**. His support has been instrumental in initiating my journey as an Authorpreneur.

Finally, heartfelt gratitude to my dedicated team – **Avesh Ansari**, **Akshay Bhat**, and **Md. Bilal** – for their unwavering support and contributions.

DEDICATION

This Book is Dedicated to My Grandparents,

R. Gangadhar & G. Vishalakshamma

And, My Dear Brother **Arvind Achar**

FOREWORD

Prof. Wg Cdr Dr. S.P. Kaushik

Dear Readers,

It is with great pleasure that I introduce the insightful book "Master Your Destiny with Numerology" by Sooraj Achar. In this enlightening read, Sooraj delves into the mystique of numerology, unraveling its profound significance in our lives.

As you embark on the journey of this book, you will discover the magical power hidden within your true potential. Sooraj brilliantly navigates through the world of numbers, explaining the intricate role they play in shaping our destinies. With a keen eye and deep understanding, he explores the nuances of numerology, demystifying questions that have intrigued many.

The beauty of this book lies in its simplicity. Sooraj has effortlessly translated complex concepts into everyday language, making the wisdom of numerology accessible to all. By understanding the significance of your date of birth, you can unlock the secrets to your strengths and weaknesses, empowering yourself to overcome challenges and embrace success.

Numerology, as Sooraj passionately asserts, is not mere superstition; it is a science, a guiding force that can transform your life. By following the principles outlined in this book, you can harness the miraculous potential within you. Sooraj's insights will not only inspire you but also provide practical tools to navigate life's journey with confidence and grace.

I wholeheartedly recommend this book to anyone seeking self-discovery, personal growth, and a deeper understanding of the profound impact numbers have on our lives. May this book be your guiding light, illuminating the path to a future filled with success, happiness, and fulfillment.

Warm regards,
Prof. Wg Cdr Dr. S.P. Kaushik
Former Director General & Pro Vice-Chancellor

K. Vikram Rastogi

This Book Inspires A Life Transformation

It is with great pleasure and enthusiasm that I introduce you to "Master Your Destiny with Numerology" by the prolific author, Sooraj Achar. I have had the privilege of knowing him personally for several years, and his dedication to the field of numerology is nothing short of inspiring. Through his 10 bestselling books, Sooraj has enlightened countless individuals on the incredible potential of numerology, and with this latest addition to his literary journey, he delves deeper into the intricacies of this ancient science to empower you to take control of your life.

As far as I am concerned, numerology had a profound impact on my life since the tender age of 18 when I had an opportunity to read the book on Numerology by Cheiro. It inspired me to acquire the admirable qualities of Abraham Lincoln and Charles Darwin, who shared my birthdate. Over the next 60 years, this influence played a significant role in shaping my character and life journey.

In today's world, where the hustle and bustle of life often distract us from the profound mysteries that surround us, numerology stands as a beacon of light. It is a testament to the fundamental truth that our lives are not mere coincidences but intricate patterns woven into the fabric of the universe. The importance of numerology cannot be understated. We have seen glimpses of this wisdom in earlier works like Cheiro's, among others, but Sooraj Achar takes us on a journey that uncovers the profound influence of numbers on our destiny.

"Master Your Destiny with Numerology" is a treasure trove of insights and revelations. Sooraj's mastery of presenting complex concepts in a simple and relatable manner shines through this book. He seamlessly weaves together the theoretical foundation of numerology with practical applications. The salient features of this book are that it contains numerous case studies that bring the subject to life. These real-life examples demonstrate how numerology can be applied to diverse aspects of our lives, including wealth, health, career, happiness, and general well-being.

Many of us often wonder how we can shape our own destiny. "Master Your Destiny with Numerology" holds the key to answering this age-old question. Through the exploration of numbers and their significance, Sooraj shows us that we have the power to influence the course of our lives. This book is not just a guide but a roadmap to understanding the intricate relationship between numbers and our personal journey. It offers practical tools and methods to align your life with the positive energies that numerology unveils.

However, it is essential to approach numerology with caution and diligence. The power of numbers is immense, and as Sooraj Achar emphasizes, the precautions to be taken for implementing the recommendations derived from numerology are critical. Numerology can reveal the hidden dynamics of our lives, but it should be approached with respect and responsibility. This book provides valuable insights on how to harness the potential of numerology without succumbing to its pitfalls.

In conclusion, "Master Your Destiny with Numerology" is a testament to Sooraj Achar's dedication to helping individuals uncover the profound wisdom that numerology holds. His work benefits not only individuals but also society at large. As we master our own destinies, we contribute to the betterment of humanity. Sooraj's teachings go beyond personal enrichment; they extend to the betterment of citizens and ultimately our entire country.

In the pages that follow, you will embark on a journey of self-discovery and empowerment. Sooraj Achar's wisdom, backed by his extensive experience and knowledge in numerology, will be your guiding light. As you delve into the depths of this book, I hope you find the answers you seek, not only for your own life but for the benefit of all human beings, citizens, and our great nation. "Master Your Destiny with Numerology" is not just a book; it is a powerful tool that has the potential to transform lives and shape destinies for the better. Enjoy the journey, and may you master your destiny with the profound wisdom of numerology.

K. Vikram Rastogi
Co-author of Secrets of Happy Healthy Long Life

KR Goswami

In the symphony of life, where the intricate notes of destiny intertwine with our choices, I stumbled upon a revelation that altered the very fabric of my existence—the profound wisdom of Numerology. It was not just any exploration, but an odyssey illuminated by the brilliance of Sooraj Achar's literary masterpiece, "Life Mastery Using Numerology."

Sooraj's narrative transcends the conventional, unlocking the celestial code that governs our destinies. The resonance of his insights echoed through the corridors of my life, transforming my understanding of Numerology from mere theory to a potent force for change. I found myself entwined with the rhythm of his words, orchestrating a symphony of transformation that extended far beyond the pages of his book.

Recently, as I embarked on the journey of aligning the energies of my newly acquired abode in Ahmedabad through Vastu, Sooraj's teachings became my guiding compass. His principles, gleaned from a profound comprehension of Numerology, manifested as an anchor amidst the swirling currents of change. Through his literary prowess, he not only imparts wisdom but also extends a helping hand to fledgling writers, nurturing the flame of creativity within them.

Sooraj Achar, a luminary in the realm of literature, is not just an author of best-selling books but a mentor and guide, selflessly fostering the growth of aspiring wordsmiths. His benevolence extends beyond the confines of his written works, as he shares the wealth of his expert knowledge with an open heart.

As a retired defense personnel akin to his father, I resonate with Sooraj's humility and soft-spoken demeanor. His words transcend the boundaries of the page, creating a bridge that connects our shared experiences and aspirations. Through his books, I discovered a mentor who not only enlightens but also uplifts—a beacon of inspiration in the vast sea of knowledge.

From the vantage point of a psychologist, I delved into the rich tapestry of Sooraj's Numerology series, captivated by the intricate dance of numbers and psychology. As a banker, immersed in the world of numbers and intricate calculations, I found solace and resonance in the harmonious blend of logic and mysticism that permeates his writings.

The transformative impact of Sooraj's Numerology books reverberates across every facet of my life, especially in the realm of relationships. It has been the cornerstone of forging unbreakable bonds with family, friends, and associates—a testament to the universality and applicability of his teachings.

Sooraj, as you embark on the journey of yet another literary masterpiece, I extend my heartfelt wishes for the success of the intellectual gems you've crafted. May your words continue to resonate across borders, shaping the intellectual landscape with international acclaim.

In gratitude and admiration,
KR Goswami
Former Aircraft Engineer, Retired Branch Manager

rcraft **Engineer, Retired Branch Manager SBI, Psychologist, Best-selling Author, and Defence recruitment trainer**

Dr. Arundhati Govind Hoskeri

Man's fascination with numbers is unique; it seems humans might have delved into counting even before mastering the art of speech! Numerology, a discipline that explores the mystical connections between life events and numbers, has been a global practice for centuries. This study carefully examines the numerical values assigned to letters, words, and names through alphanumeric systems.

It's heartening to see a growing interest among educated youth in this divinatory art and science of Numerology. Sooraj Achar, a Software Engineer, has immersed himself deeply in the study of Numerology and is now generously sharing his knowledge with others.

In his latest book, "Master Your Destiny With Numerology," Sooraj not only imparts fundamental knowledge accessible to a layman but also provides a comprehensive, step-by-step guide to help readers carve their paths toward desired goals and success.

The book seamlessly integrates Eastern and Western perspectives on number divination, delving into the influence of planets associated with each number and their vibrations on individuals. Sooraj offers corrective measures to strengthen these vibrations, facilitating the achievement of desired results.

An intriguing aspect of the book is Sooraj's exploration of a 4000-year-old Chinese Numerology known as the "Lo Shu Grid," presented in a manner that is easy to study and comprehend.

Readers will discover their Destiny Numbers and Life Path Numbers and learn to resonate positively with their names, phone numbers, cars, lottery tickets, journeys, and practically everything else.

Sooraj's meticulous research and profound understanding of the subject are evident throughout the book. I'm confident that readers will greatly benefit from his wealth of knowledge. I wish Sooraj Achar all the very best for this exciting new venture!

Dr Arundhati Govind Hoskeri
MSc, MEd, MA (English Literature), PhD, ACTL
Diploma in Public Speaking (Trinity College of London),
NDHS(Doctor of Natural Health Sciences)
Educational Consultant for Cambridge International
Schools
Former Director and Principal of Cambridge
International School and I B World School

Dr. P. NEELA

"MASTER YOUR DESTINY WITH NUMEROLOGY" by **Sooraj Achar**

Numerology is the ancient study of numbers and their meanings. It has been used for centuries to understand the human personality, predict the future, and make better decisions in life.

In his book, "MASTER YOUR DESTINY WITH NUMEROLOGY," Sooraj Achar provides a comprehensive and practical guide to using numerology to transform your life. He covers all basic and essential aspects of numerology, including:

- How to calculate your life path number, destiny number, soul urge number, and personality number

- What does each number mean and how does it influence your life

- How to use numerology to find your strengths and weaknesses, identify your life purpose, and make better choices

- How to use numerology to improve your relationships, finances, and overall well-being

Achar also provides a number of simple and effective remedies that you can use to address any challenges you may be facing in your life.

Whether you are a beginner or an experienced numerologist, "MASTER YOUR DESTINY WITH NUMEROLOGY" is an essential resource for anyone who wants to use the power of numbers to create the life they desire.

Some specific benefits that you can expect to gain from reading this book include personal transformation harmonious relationships, financial abundance, self-discovery, etc,

If you are ready to take control of your destiny and create the life you desire, then "MASTER YOUR DESTINY WITH NUMEROLOGY" is the book for you. Sooraj Achar provides a clear and concise guide to using numerology to transform your life in all areas. I wish you all success!!!

Dr. P. NEELA
Josh Talks Speaker

CONTENTS

YOUR NEXT UNFORGETTABLE ADVENTURE BEGINS HERE!

2. Master Your NAME-SPELLING With Numerology

3. Master Your RELATIONSHIPS With Numerology

4. Master Your MONEY With Numerology

5. Master Your HEALTH With Numerology

 **6. Master Your PROFESSIONAL GOALS With Numerology**

Series-2: Master Your Life with VASTU

 **1. Master Your DESTINY With Vastu**

 **2. Master Your HOME HARMONY With Vastu**

 **3. Master Your WEALTH With Vastu**

 **4. Master Your CAREER With Vastu**

 **5. Master Your HEALTH With Vastu**

 **6. Master Your RELATIONSHIPS With Vastu**

Series-3: The Ultimate Self-Healing Mastery

 **1. Discover Your Life Purpose**

 **2. The Alchemy Of Healing**

 **3. The Essence of MINDFUL LIVING**

<u>Series-4:</u> Energize Your Mind, Body & Soul

 **1. The Art of Balancing YIN-YANG Energy**

 **2. The Art of Mastering FEARLESS MINDSET**

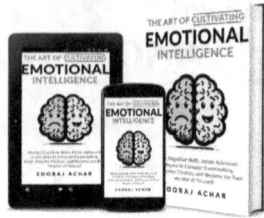 **3. The Art of Cultivating EMOTIONAL INTELLIGENCE**

 **4. The 7 Energy Needs**

5. The Power Of ONE Question

Series-5: Achieve Life-Mastery with the NUMEROLOGY Bundle

1. Master Your DESTINY & NAME-SPELLING With Numerology

2. Master Your HEALTH & RELATIONSHIPS With Numerology

3. Master Your MONEY & PROFESSIONAL GOALS With Numerology

Series-6: <u>Achieve Life Mastery with the Vastu Bundle</u>

 **1. Master Your DESTINY And CAREER With Vastu: 2 Books in 1**

 **2. Master Your HOME HARMONY And WEALTH With Vastu: 2 Books in 1**

 **3. Master Your HEALTH And RELATIONSHIPS With Vastu: 2 Books in 1**

IMPORTANT! - BEFORE YOU PROCEED

Important Note to Readers

D ear Reader,

Before embarking on the insightful journey presented in this book, "Master Your MONEY With Numerology," we highly recommend delving into the foundational knowledge provided in the first six chapters of the Numerology Mastery series – "Master Your DESTINY With Numerology." These initial chapters serve as the cornerstone for understanding the core principles and concepts that underpin the world of numerology.

In "Master Your DESTINY With Numerology," we unravel the mysteries of numerology, exploring the profound connections between your date of birth and the intricate tapestry of your life. The insights gained from these foundational chapters will lay a robust groundwork for comprehending the advanced concepts and applications discussed in this present volume.

Kindly Download Your "Free Book" Here By Scanning the QR Code Click the Link Below:

"FREE MASTERY BOOK"

The mastery of numerology is a progressive journey, much like building a house where a sturdy foundation ensures the strength and stability of the entire structure. Likewise, the knowledge gained from the initial chapters acts as the bedrock, enhancing your ability to grasp the intricacies of financial empowerment explored in "Master Your MONEY With Numerology."

By familiarizing yourself with the foundational principles, you'll be better equipped to extract maximum value from the advanced techniques, personalized analyses, and strategic insights presented in subsequent chapters. We encourage you to absorb the wisdom shared in the earlier segments to fully harness the transformative potential that numerology offers on your path to financial mastery.

Thank you for your commitment to self-discovery and empowerment through numerology.

Wishing you an enriching and enlightening reading experience.

Warm regards,
Sooraj Achar
Author, Numerology Mastery Series

DO YOU WANT ME TO PERSONALLY HELP?

BOOK A FREE 30-MINUTE NUMEROLOGY CONSULTATION

You're invited to book a **free 30-minute one-on-one consultation** with renowned Numerology and Vastu Coach and Consultant, Sooraj Achar. This personalized session will help you understand your Numerology birth chart and reveal your strengths, weaknesses, and more. Also get an opportunity to apply for your Detailed Numerology Fortune Report.

Topics Covered in Your Detailed Numerology Fortune Report:

1. Detailed Characteristics

2. What Your Driver-Conductor Combination Says About You

3. Insights from the Yogas in Your DOB

Free Bonuses:

- 10 **Numerology Books Bundle**, covering 100+ unique topics

- 2 **Free 1-2-1 Consultations**

"Free 30-Minute Numerology Consultation"

Ready to Talk? Click the Link Above or Scan the **QR Code** Below to Book a Free Call

Don't miss this opportunity to gain profound insights into your life. Book your free consultation today and claim your detailed Numerology report.

HOW THIS BOOK CAN WORK MIRACLES IN YOUR LIFE?

*"Change your numbers, change your energy,
change your life."* - Sooraj Achar

Introduction: What If One Book Could Shift Your Entire Financial Destiny?

Have you ever felt like you're working harder than ever, yet success seems just out of reach?
Do you wonder why some people effortlessly attract wealth and prosperity while others struggle despite their talent?
What if your financial breakthrough wasn't in your efforts alone—but hidden in your **birth chart's secret code**?

You're holding a book that doesn't just give you more information. It gives you a **transformation**.
One that begins with *awareness* and ends with *abundance*.

This book is your *numerical compass*. A tool unlike any other, designed to unlock the hidden blueprint of your financial life. The moment you open yourself to its teachings, miracles start to happen—not because of magic, but because of **mathematical precision aligned with universal energy**.

Let's walk through how this book can rewire your financial destiny from the inside out.

Why This Book Isn't Just Information—It's Financial Transformation

Too many people read self-help books, feel a temporary spark, and then—nothing changes. Why? Because most books give **ideas**. This book gives you a **system**. A system rooted in ancient Lo Shu Grid wisdom and modern Numerology science, revealing:

- **Where your money blockages live**

- **Which numbers attract abundance or repel it**

- **What kind of financial opportunities you're naturally aligned with**

- **How to reprogram your money mindset at the identity level**

- **How to predict and prepare for your next money wave**

Let's face it—working harder is no longer the answer. **Working smarter with energy intelligence** is.

And that's where this book becomes your secret financial weapon.

What You'll Gain from Reading and Applying This Book

This isn't theory. These are **tangible, measurable, repeatable results** when you take action on this system:

1. Deep Financial Clarity

You'll finally understand your **financial DNA**—what works for you, what sabotages you, and why.

2. Elimination of Hidden Money Blocks

Using the Lo Shu Grid and karmic patterns, you'll detect and dissolve deep-rooted financial limitations passed down from family or past lives.

3. Predictive Financial Power

No more guessing. You'll discover when to launch, invest, buy property, or hold back—backed by numbers, not luck.

4. Instant Identity Shift

You'll stop saying, "I'm not good with money." Instead, you'll **become a magnet for wealth**—through a new, numerically-aligned self-concept.

5. Energetic Alignment with Wealth

From your **home number to your car** to your name vibration—every piece of your environment will align with prosperity.

6. Rapid Results with a 10-Minute Daily Practice

You don't need to meditate for hours. With short, focused steps, you'll **install success frequency into your mind and numbers daily**.

Life-Changing Books That Have Influenced Millions

If you're on a path of transformation, you've likely come across classics like:

- *Think and Grow Rich* by Napoleon Hill

- *The Secret* by Rhonda Byrne

- *You Are a Badass at Making Money* by Jen Sincero

- *Breaking the Habit of Being Yourself* by Dr. Joe Dispenza

- *The Power of Your Subconscious Mind* by Dr. Joseph Murphy

- *Atomic Habits* by James Clear

- *The Psychology of Money* by Morgan Housel

These books are powerful. They teach the **mindset** and **belief** elements of success. But here's where this book goes beyond.

What Makes This Book *Better, Faster, and Easier* Than Others?

Simple: No Complex Calculations or Astrology Charts

You don't need to be a math genius or Vedic scholar. If you can count from 1 to 9, you can decode your financial chart.

Fast: 10-Minute Daily System

This isn't a read-once-and-forget book. It gives you **practical micro-routines** to shift your money frequency in under 10 minutes a day.

Specific: Laser-Focused on *Money Mastery*

While other books generalize about success or mindset, this book directly targets your **wealth code, money blocks, property energy, and stock timing**.

Personal: Tailored to *Your Unique Birth Chart*

Unlike one-size-fits-all advice, this book personalizes every insight based on your **Lo Shu Grid**, **birth numbers**, and **environmental numerology**.

Proven: Rooted in Ancient Wisdom and Modern Results

Used by kings, monks, and millionaires—the **Lo Shu system** has stood the test of centuries. Now, it's adapted for today's fast-paced financial world.

Who Is This Book For?

Whether you're a:

- **Student** confused about your career direction

- **Entrepreneur** seeking to align business energy for income leaps

- **Professional** stuck in the same income bracket

- **Parent** trying to build legacy wealth

- **Investor** looking for optimal buying/selling cycles

- Or simply someone who knows you're *meant for more*—

This book is your financial decoder.

Real-Life Miracles You Can Expect

After working with thousands of Numerology and Vastu clients, here are just a few transformations readers experience:

- Property that had been stuck for 2+ years sold in 21

days after correcting the home number vibration

- Business owners 3X'ed their monthly income after aligning their name and brand numerology

- Individuals with poor saving habits finally created wealth discipline using their daily number

- Investors timed their stock market entries using their personal wealth period and Lo Shu blueprint

- Clients bought their first dream home—aligned with personal money years and favorable directions

Miracles don't come from chance. They come from numeric precision.

Conclusion: Your Journey to Financial Freedom Starts Now

You didn't land on this book by accident. You were *drawn* to it by resonance—because a part of you is ready.

Ready to step beyond the "work harder" trap.
Ready to say goodbye to scarcity, anxiety, and confusion.
Ready to finally **master your money with Numerology**.

This book will not only give you the **how** but also the **why** behind your past struggles—and the exact **next steps** to attract wealth and protect it.

So here's what you must do: **Commit. Read. Apply. Align.** And most importantly—**watch the miracles unfold.**

Let's make your **money story a masterpiece**.

CHAPTER 1

HOW TO DETECT MONEY SECTOR?

"In the world of numbers, lies the key to unlocking the doors of financial prosperity. Master Your MONEY With Numerology and open the gateway to abundance." – **Sooraj Achar**

U nlocking the secrets to financial prosperity begins with understanding the Money Sector in numerology. Delve into this chapter as we explore the mystical realms of numbers, discovering the key indicators and insights that guide you toward wealth and abundance. Prepare to decipher the language of numerology and unveil the path to financial success hidden within the digits of your existence.

Let's begin, we will learn what is in our date of birth, and what is the function of the 8 types of Lines and Yogas. What these Yogas tell us about our personality and our traits. In this topic, we learn some attributes and how these lines tell about your Strengths, Weaknesses, Health, Wealth, and Prosperity.

Note: "Yoga" is a term that originates from the ancient Sanskrit language of India. In English, "yoga" is used to describe a set of physical, mental, and spiritual practices that aim to promote overall well-being and harmony. The word itself can be translated to mean "union" or "discipline," reflecting the holistic nature of yoga that aligns mind, body, and spirit.

So, let's begin with the new topic- **8 Yogas in Numerology**

What is my meaning of this? For reference, refer to the Loshu grid.

4 RAHU	9 MARS	2 MOON
3 JUPITER	5 MERCURY	7 KETU
8 SATURN	1 SUN	6 VENUS

As I told you earlier, there are 8 types of lines and yogas. 3 vertical, 3 horizontal, and 2 diagonal lines.

4, 3, 8 is first, 9, 5, 1 is second, and 2, 7, 6 is the third vertical. And so on you can check for horizontal and diagonal lines. What do these lines tell us?

First of all, let's see three **Vertical Planes/Lines**.

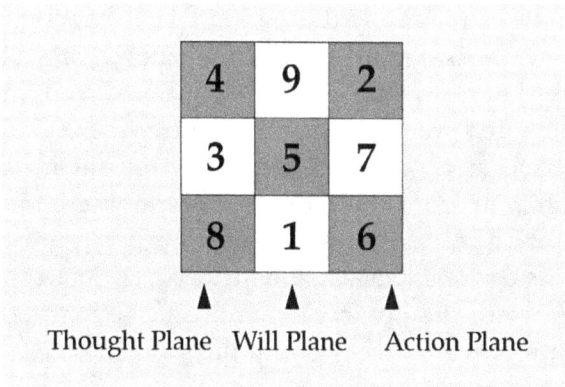

Thought Plane   Will Plane   Action Plane

Our first vertical line is 4, 3, and 8. The first vertical line of someone's numeroscope is called the **"Thought Plane"** and if 4, 3, 8 are present in that plane it means that the thought process of that person is very strong. This type of person has an extreme ability to think. They are also prudent. You may have seen a person saying that we should buy this property now for 5 lakhs and after 10 years it will be valued at 50 lakhs. And after 10 years, you see that the property is actually having a value of 50 lakhs. Because this type of person has a different vision, which he has the ability to predict. This type of person is rich in discipline, organization, and visualization.

After 4, 3, 8 our next plane is 9, 5, 1, and it is called the **"Will Plane"**.

Persons who are born in the last century 9 and 1 are common in everyone's date of birth. So 9 and 1 is not going to make any difference in this particular plane. So which number is going to make the difference? Remember, number 5 is going to make the difference. 5 is the soul of this "will plane". If someone has 9, 5, and 1, I will say his willpower is very strong. In a single line, I will say these people are the real fighters. This type of person can handle extremely hard situations. They have the ability to bounce back again and again whenever they are out of track. They can fight physical, emotional, and financial problems. It is very difficult to identify these people by seeing their faces. They are different from the inside and look different from the outside. They look the same, no matter if they are happy or sad. Because number 5 is balancing their personality and life between 9 and 1. If you correlate with the numbers of your life, you can see how these numbers are affecting your life.

So let's move forward.

2, 7, and 6 is our third vertical line. It is called the **"Action Plane"**. I shared with you one numeroscope example in our last chapter, in which you can see that the numbers 2, 7, 6 are present in the numeroscope. So you can say that he is an action-oriented person. Action-oriented meaning is that if this type of person makes a decision in their life, it is next to impossible they will not act.

Let me explain to you, with an example.

If this type of person goes to a shop and sees a pen there and likes the pen worth Rs. 50. They will immediately buy the pen when they know that they can find the same pen for Rs 40 in another shop. Once they make up their mind, they will not delay, they will just act. If someone has 2, 7, 6 he/she can't control their excitement. They are always excited about life. Their decision may be right or wrong, but they will definitely convert it into action.

These were all three vertical lines.

Now we have 4, 9, and 2 in our first **Horizontal Plane/Line** and it is called the **"Mental Plane"**.

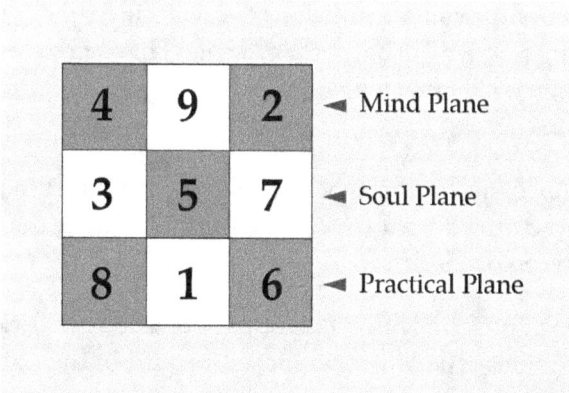

9 are common for all born in the last century and 2 are common for all born in this century. If these three numbers are present in someone's numeroscope, I will say in one line that they are people with God-gifted brains. They can remember everything they see. They are mentally very strong and they have a very sharp memory. This type of person is very intelligent and they can process intellectual capability. Suppose there are 10 people, 9 people are going in the same direction; this one will go the other way. And after some time, they will all realize that this person is going in the right direction.

The next three numbers on our second horizontal plane are 3, 5, and 7 and it is called the **"Emotional/Soul Plane"**. These people are ruled by their emotions. Their heart rules over their brain. This type of person is golden-hearted. They believe very easily, they trust anyone very easily. And they may fall into trouble because of this nature.

Let's see an example.

If a person comes to this type of person for help. The person had cheated them twice; they will still help this person knowing that he will cheat them again. They know that they are going to fall into trouble again, but they can't control their emotions.

The punch line for this type of people is- their heart rules over their head, they are trustworthy people and they are the people with the golden heart.

The next horizontal line is 8, 1, 6, and it is called the **"Practical Plane"**. This type of person moves forward in their life with a practical approach. When you talk to this type of person or you discuss a project with them, they will ask what? why? When? Where? How?

They like to go into the depth of things. They have an analytical brain. They approach everything in a logical and scientific way. It is very difficult to teach this type of people; it is very difficult to win logically from this type of people.

Suppose you are asking this type of person to go with you on a tour. He will ask you- what is the departure time? What is the mode of transfer? Are we going by airplane or train or bus? What would be the budget?

What type of weather is there? And after asking too many things, they will decide whether to go or not. It means they are going through details, details, and details, then they are deciding whether to take action or not.

Hope you are enjoying this.

Now let's move forward to two **Diagonal Planes**.

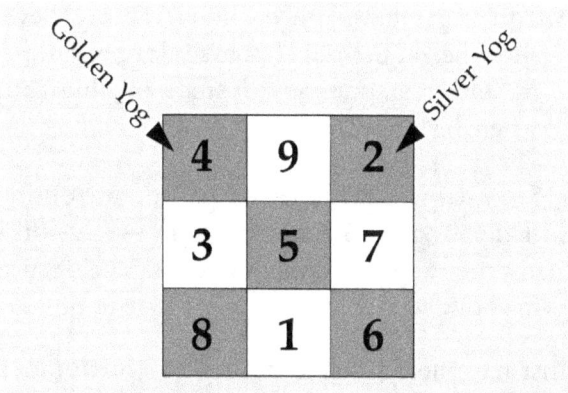

Our first Diagonal Plane is 4, 5, and 6, called the **"Super Success Line"**. In our Hindu mythology, it is known as **"Raj Yoga/Golden Yoga"**. You will rarely find a person containing these three numbers in their numeroscope. These types of people get super successful in their lives. They have a large figure of money. They have the fame, they have the name and they are on a higher level. If you have 4, 5, and 6 in your numeroscope, you are opting to be successful in your life.

I have some examples:

- Baba Ramdev- is a simple common man, and he does not have any degree, but you can see where he is.

- Shri Shri Ravishankar

- Amir Khan

- Sonia Gandhi

- Sanjay Lila Bhansali

- Anil Kapoor

- You must have heard about Johnny Lever- is a short-height person. His physical appearance is not so mesmerizing, but you can see from a bus conductor where he is now.

So if 4, 5, 6 are in your numeroscope, you are opting to be successful. If you have 4, 5, 6 and you are not successful, believe me, you just need a spark. You are very near to being successful. If this is in your date of birth, you must have to be successful.

You must have heard that after a child's birth in a family, the parents become very successful. It happened because the child was containing 4, 5, 6 and he will get his success, his luxury through his parents. Even his father doesn't have a good numeroscope. You must have heard that after getting married, a person becomes more successful. These are the common examples you must have observed in your life.

Our last line, our next diagonal line is 2, 5, 8, and it is called the **"Success Line/Silver Yoga"**.

It is different from the super success line. If you have these numbers, you are also opting to be successful. We also call 2, 5, 8 the **earth elements**. This person will have his own house in the early stage of his life. They are successful in the property business. They get benefits from real estate. They invest a little in the property and get a large profit from it. According to the earth elements, they are also successful in the agricultural field and farming.

We are done with all 8 lines and I hope you understood each and every line very well.

I want to repeat one line again.

9, 5, 1 - first I named it **"will plane"**. It is also called the **"symbol of success"**.

If you don't have 4, 5, and 6, and if you also don't have 2, 5, 8, but you have 9, 5, and 1. You deserve to be successful. If you are still not successful, there are some missing things we will talk about in our next lectures. 70- 80% of successful people have common factors 9, 5, 1 in their numeroscope. You can check for Bill Gates, Warren Buffett, Jeff Bezos, Mukesh Ambani, and Sri Sri Ravi Shankar.

There may be a question in your mind that if someone doesn't have all three numbers or they have only two numbers or they have only one number or they do not have any of these numbers, then what will happen?

Let me show you the same example: date of birth, which is 13 Feb 1967. After making the numeroscope, in the first vertical line, you can see that the number 8 is missing and in the second vertical line, the number 5 is missing. And if I see the eight yogas, he has only two yogas 4, 9, 2, and 2, 7, 6.

When we talk about strength, we will check for fully completed lines. If the lines are complete, they are your **strengths,** and if the lines are incomplete, they are your **weaknesses**. If you can identify your strengths and your weaknesses, it will be very easy to navigate your life. But don't worry if you have many incomplete lines, because you will know how to navigate your life in the next chapters. You saw that a line can contain all three or double or single numbers. Now we will see if, in a single block, there are numbers in pairs.

For example, Let's talk about 438. How many pairs it will form: (4, 3) (3, 8) (8, 4)

If there are 4, 3, and 8, I will say that your thought plane is giving you 100% power and your plane is excellent. And if only two numbers/a pair are present, I will say it is giving you 66% power and your plane is good. And if there is only one number present, I will say it is giving you 33% power and your plane is okay.

If not a single number is present, then I will say your plane is weak, and it is not giving you any power. But it is possible that your other planes may be strong. If you do not have these numbers, you can still have success in your life because you are able to navigate. We will learn how to explore whatever numbers we have.

We will learn how we can fill the gaps of missing numbers and how we can use repeating numbers. We have all the tools to increase the ratings of your date of birth. We will learn them all from our previous books.

Role of Lotteries in Birth Chart

There are three types of lotteries in a date of birth:

1. Driver No.

2. Conductor No.

3. Kua No.

Are they really lotteries? And why am I calling them lotteries?

A lottery represents a substantial and unexpected prize that can dramatically alter our future. During our childhood, we often engaged in activities akin to lotteries, which involved scratching a board with immense excitement to reveal a number. Depending on the revealed number, we received prizes such as marbles, toffees, or toys.

You can encounter a similar level of excitement when examining your date of birth (DOB). It's important to note that not everyone possesses all three "lotteries" within their DOB. Some may have only one, others might have two, and a fortunate few may possess all three, while some may have none of them.

Finding Lotteries:

For example, assume a dob is 13-02-1967.

In the above-mentioned DOB, the driver is 4, conductor is 2 and Kua is 6. Now we need to check how many lotteries are there in this dob. First of all, we need to make the chart.

Now when you go to fill number 4 (driver) in the chart you will find that the block of number 4 is empty. As you fill the number 4 in the chart the line of 4-9-2 gets completed.

"If the number of your driver is not already there in your DOB it means you have the lottery of Diver."

Now we will fill the number 2 (conductor) in the birth chart, but it is already there from the date of birth. If your conductor number is already there in your chart from your date of birth it means you don't have the lottery of conductor.

Now we will check for the Kua number. In our example, the Kua number is 6, which is already present in the DOB. It means this DOB does not have the lottery of Kua number.

"In simple words, if your driver, conductor, and Kua number is not directly present in your date of birth it means you have the lottery of that particular number."

In our example (13-02-1967) there is only one lottery present which is the lottery of Driver number. The driver number is 4 which is not present in the DOB therefore it has the lottery of driver.

Power of Lottery:

If your lottery number completes a line in your chart, it is a very powerful lottery. It's not actually a Lottery, it is a Jackpot now.

Now assume another DOB, 31-01-1968. This is an exercise for you to make its chart and find out lotteries in this DOB. This DOB has all three lotteries. For this DOB the Driver is 4, Conductor is 2 and Kua is 5. Lines of 2-5-8, 4-5-6, and 9-5-1 are complete in this DOB, this person is born with SUPER RAJ YOG.

That's all for now!

CHAPTER 2

COMMON FACTOR AMONG RICH & SUCCESSFUL PEOPLE

"Numerology is the science of the soul and its evolution, and numbers are the key to unlocking the secrets of our inner selves."
- Dr. R.G. Srinivasan

What do all the richest people have in common that leads them to great success? This common factor might also be in your date of birth (DOB), even if you don't know it. Our goal is to discover this potential in our DOB and use it to achieve maximum success in life.

"That common factor is **9-5-1.**" If these three numbers are present in your DOB, it signifies that you are destined for success. For example, consider a DOB of 27-05-1957; since all three numbers are present, it suggests that this person is predisposed to be successful.

Now, let's delve into the DOBs of some of the richest individuals. Jeff Bezos, the owner of Amazon, possesses these three numbers in his DOB. Mukesh Ambani, the richest person in India, also has these three numbers in his DOB. Ratan Tata, a respected figure in business, shares this commonality. Bollywood luminaries such as Sanjay Leela Bhansali, Salman Khan, Shah Rukh Khan, and Aamir Khan all have these three numbers in their DOBs.

Number 9 represents Mars, endowing individuals with power, direction, and the strength to persevere. Number 5 is associated with Mercury, providing balance, wisdom, and knowledge. Lastly, the number 1 symbolizes the Sun, the number of the King. With qualities akin to a king, the balance of Mercury, and the spirit of Mars, success becomes an inevitable outcome. If you have these three you have to be successful but your intention should be good and your goal should be clear.

CHAPTER 3
POWER OF NUMBER 6: VENUS

*"Numerology is the study of the hidden meanings
behind numbers, and how they can reveal
important information about an individual's
personality and destiny."*
- Dr. David Palmer

Today's era is the era of Venus. Everyone wants to be rich, everyone desires a substantial bank balance, and everyone aspires to live a life filled with luxury and glamour. In this chapter, we will discuss the uplifting of Venus. I will share methods to uplift this planet and provide deeper insights into this subject.

The number associated with Venus is 6, and it represents the color white. If you want to uplift Venus, or if either your driver or conductor is 6, or if you don't have the number 6 in your birth chart, you should follow these remedies. However, ensure that neither your driver nor conductor is 3, as 3 is the number of Jupiter, which is antagonistic to Venus.

Remedies:

1. Donate white items such as clothes, sweets, rice, and milk on Fridays to the disabled or needy. You can also distribute kheer made by yourself to the disabled or needy on Fridays.

2. Always keep something white with you. This could be wearing white clothes, carrying a white handkerchief, wearing a white band on your wrist, wearing white undergarments, carrying a pen with a white body, or wearing white-framed glasses.

3. If you are unable to find the poor or disabled, you can donate white items to temples and gurudwaras.

Precautions:

If your driver or conductor is 6, stay away from yellow. Avoid the color yellow as much as possible, as it is associated with Jupiter, which is Venus's antagonist.

Conclusion:

In conclusion, embracing the energy of Venus and aligning ourselves with its positive influences can bring prosperity and harmony into our lives. By incorporating the suggested remedies and precautions, we can work towards uplifting the Venusian aspects within us. Remember, the pursuit of wealth and luxury is not just a materialistic endeavor; it is an alignment with the cosmic forces that govern our existence.

As we navigate the cosmic dance of planets and their energies, may the radiance of Venus illuminate our paths and lead us towards a life adorned with abundance and grace. Let the color white symbolize not only purity but also the purity of intentions as we strive for personal and collective upliftment. May the celestial harmony of Venus guide us in creating a life that reflects the beauty and balance of the cosmos.

CHAPTER 4

UNLOCKING THE FUTURE: PREDICTIONS BEYOND THE DATE OF BIRTH

*"Numerology is the study of the power and meaning behind numbers and their influence on our lives." - **Dr. Michael Losier***

You may know many people who don't know their date of birth. They don't even know their birth month and year. In that case, how we can predict their life, we will learn in this chapter?

Only use this tool when there is a doubt about the date of birth. If you know the exact date, don't use this tool.

Let's take a hypothetical example.

Suppose we have a client who doesn't know his date of birth and he is asking- **"will I be able to get my house in 2020?"**

We will answer this question through the pyramid of numbers. In his question (will I be able to get my house in 2020?).

Word count in question:

will I be able to get my house in 2020?

1 2 3 4 5 6 7   8 9 10

There are a total of 10 words. The total of 10 is 1. Now count the number of letters in each word.

Counting letters in each word:

will I be able to get my house in 2020?

4 1 2 4 2 3 2   5 2 4

And write them near this 1 (total of words).

1 4 1 2 4 2 3 2 5 2 4

Now we will add two adjacent numbers. Until we get a single-digit number.

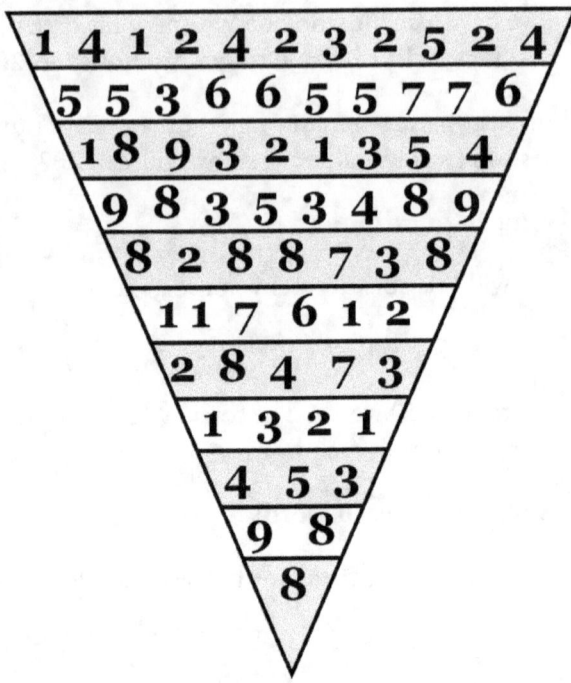

That's how we end up with 8.

So your question will become a number at the end.

Now we need to find the answer. The answer would be a yes or no. We can find this with the help of this table.

Number	Answer
1	Yes
2	No
3	Yes
4	No
5	Yes
6	Yes
7	No
8	No
9	Yes: No 50:50

According to the table answer to our client's question is **NO** (according to the pyramid question's numerical value was one).

This is the method by which you can make predictions without knowing someone's date of birth. All you need to do is- figure out a single-digit number with the pyramid method from the question of the client and match this with the table and you will find whether the answer is yes or no.

CHAPTER 5

JACKPOT: BIG ARROWS AND SMALL ARROWS

*"Numbers are more than symbols; they are the silent architects of our financial destiny. Let this book be your guide to understanding the numerical language of wealth." – **Sooraj Achar***

I told you about 8 types of lines and yogas in the Loshu Grid. There were three verticals, 3 horizontals, and two diagonal lines. Arrows are a different view of those lines. Same as lines, we have 3 Vertical, 3 horizontal, and 2 Diagonal Arrows.

BIG ARROWS

1. Vertical Arrows: Observe the below Loshu Grid

4 RAHU	9 MARS	2 MOON
3 JUPITER	5 MERCURY	7 KETU
8 SATURN	1 SUN	6 VENUS

4,3,8 - Planners, Shrewd, Cunning
9,5,1 - Decision-Makers
2,7,6 - Always grab opportunities, very good at Sports

If number 4, 3, and 8 is present in your numeroscope, it is called the **"Planner Arrow"**. This type of person is very good at planning. It is also called the **"Politician Arrow"**. If someone wants to go into politics, it is the most important arrow for them. These people can be cunning and shrewd as well.

If 9, 5, and 1 are present in someone's chart, they are very good decision-makers. Their willpower is very strong. They are the fighters and they have the ability to bounce back. If numbers 2, 7, and 6 are present in someone's chart, they know how to grab an opportunity. They are also very good at sports. If someone wants to go into physical sports, this is the perfect arrow.

2. Horizontal Arrows: Observe the below Loshu Grid

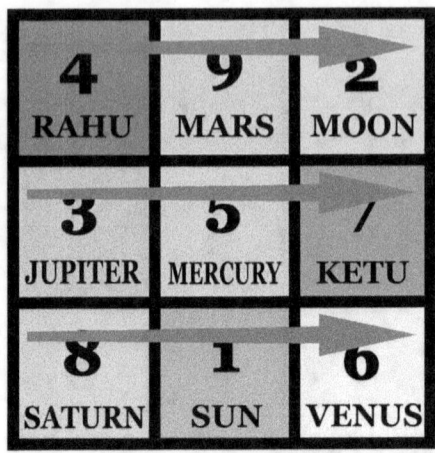

4,9,2 - Sharp Memory, Intellectual
3,5,7 - Golden heart, Emotional, Spiritual, religious, god loving, Compassionate
8,1,6 - Arrow of Prosperity

If someone has 4, 9, and 2 in their chart, they have a very sharp memory. They have an intellectual brain. They want to do something different.

If someone has the numbers 3, 5, and 7 (Jupiter, Mercury, and Ketu) in their chart, they are the people with the golden heart. These are the people who are very, very compassionate. They are kind to others and they always help people in need. They can be religious and spiritual. They always move around religious people (monks/priests) and temples. If 8,1 and 6 are present in someone's chart, it is called the **Arrow of Prosperity**. We called them a very **Practical Arrow**. Yes! They are practical, but at the same time; they have prosperity. They are also very successful in their life.

3. Diagonal Arrows: Observe the below Loshu Grid

4,5,6 - Aggressive, Balanced, Rich

2,5,8 - Very Patient, wait for the right moment to act, and never lose sight of their goal.

If someone has 4,5,6 in the chart, they are very aggressive towards things. They have a good balance in their life and ultimately they are rich. No one can stop a person if he has aggression and balance both at the same time.

If someone has 2,5,8 in their chart, we discussed before that they are good at property business. These people are very, very patient.

They never hustle and they wait for the right moment to act. They never lose sight of their goal. When they find the right moment, they hit their goal.

They are the same as Arjun in Mahabharat, always looking at the bird's eyes.

SMALL ARROWS

Observe the below Loshu Grid:

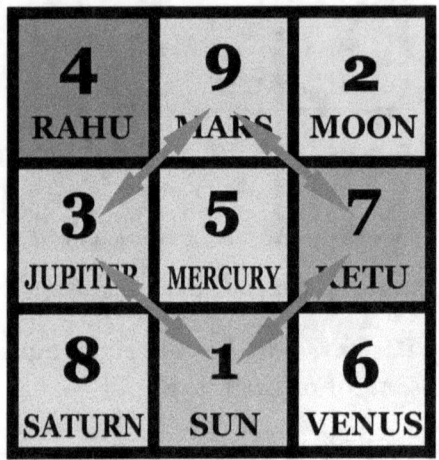

These arrows are not so important, but they may be useful sometimes. These arrows are formed by 9, 7, 1, and 3.

9,7 - Keep balance in difficult situations

7,1 - Go into Deep Research

3,1 - Spiritual, Knowledgeable, Intelligent

3,9 - Litigation, Argumentative

If 9 and 7 are present in someone's chart, they always keep the balance even in very difficult situations. Number 9 is the number of aggression and 7 is the number of spiritualism. That's why they know how to handle difficult situations.

If 7 and 1 Sun and Ketu are present in someone's chart, they are very good at deep research. They can do very well at the occult or Ph.D.

If someone has 3 and 1 (Jupiter and Sun) present in their chart, they are very good at the occult, spiritualism, religion, and knowledge. They are very intelligent as well.

If someone has three and nine in their chart, it is called the Arrow of Litigation and Argumentation. These people are very argumentative about little things. These people have to face many court cases in their lives.

CHAPTER 6

A GUIDE TO HOUSE NUMBERS & REMEDIAL MEASURES

"Your financial journey is written in the language of numbers. Decode the secrets of wealth with Master Your MONEY With Numerology and script a tale of enduring prosperity."
– Sooraj Achar

I n this chapter, we will learn how to calculate a perfect house number, flat number, tower number, or block number for our sweet home.

Case 1:

In many residential colonies, house numbers start with alphabets, e.g., A/512, B/654, C/357, etc. So the question is: does this alphabet interrupt the house number? Do we need to add its numerical value to our house number? Let's understand with an example:

Suppose a house number is A/512. In this case, 'A' represents the block, and 512 is the house number within that block. The block 'A' can have about 100 to 200 houses, which means 'A' is fixed for all the houses, and 'A' remains static for each house while the number changes. It means only the number is variable, not the alphabet. In this case, we will not include 'A' because it's static. So the number for A/512 depends only on 512, which equals 5+1+2 = 8. Similarly, the number for B/654 will be 6+5+4 = 15 and further reduced to 1+5 = 6.

Case 2:

Some houses have this alphabetical character at the end of their house number, e.g., 512A, 654B, etc. This usually occurs when a large plot is divided into two or three smaller plots. Suppose there was a plot numbered 512, and the builder divided it into three smaller plots. Now, he cannot assign the numbers 513 and 514 to these new plots because those numbers are already allocated to adjacent plots. Therefore, the builder designates these plots as 512A, 512B, and 512C. In this case, do we need to calculate the numerical value of the alphabet? Let's understand with an example:

In these cases, the number (i.e., 512) is static, and the alphabets are variable. So, we have to calculate the numerical value of the alphabet. If the house number is 512A, it will be calculated as 5+1+2+1 = 9, where the last 1 represents the value of 'A'. Similarly, if the house number is 719C, it will be calculated as 7+1+9+3 = 20, which further simplifies to 2+0 = 2. In this case, the last 3 represent the position of the letter 'C' in the English alphabet.

Case 3:

Many houses have '/' in their house number, e.g., 16/24, 19/32, etc. It can be very confusing to determine which number is the house number and which one is the block number. In this case, I will ask my client to provide the house numbers of their previous or next houses to determine which number is the static block number and which one is the variable house number.

For example, the next houses of 16/24 can be 16/25, 16/26, 16/27. In this case, 16 is the block number, which is static, and the other number is the house number. Similarly, in example two, the next houses of 16/24 can be 17/24, 18/24, 19/24. In this case, 24 is the block number, which is static, and the other number is the house number, which is variable.

If you have a tower number, you don't need to include it in the calculation. If your house is in tower 2 and the flat number is 409, your house number will be 4+0+9 = 13, which further simplifies to 1+3 = 4.

The formula is that we won't calculate the static number; it doesn't make any impact. We only need to calculate the changing number.

Remedies for Wrong House Number

What are the Wrong House numbers?

We call it a wrong house number when it is not according to numerology

- it can be on a struggling number like 4 or 8.

- Or it is also possible that your house number is not syncing with your date of birth. As your driver number is 6 and house number is 3 and vice versa.

- Another possibility is that your house number is 18 or 36 which are struggling numbers.

Example:

Suppose your house number is A/62, its numerology number will be 6+2=8, which is a struggling number. Now how can we fix it?

The best way to dilute its effect is to not display this number on the nameplate outside your house.

If you are not able to do so, due to some reasons if you have to display the number, you can follow these remedies:-

1. In the first step add '-' or '/' between the number and the alphabet. This will look like this- A-62 or A/62

2. Write the alphabet slightly blurred, it should be less visible than the number.

31

3. Write the entire number (including the alphabet) on a green circle. This circle will capture its effect and it will not affect you.

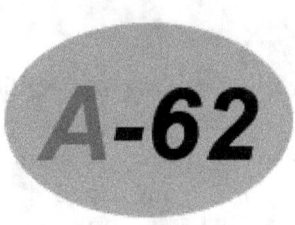

If your House number is **62A:**

In this case, we need to follow the same steps as above.

1. Add '-' or '/' between.

2. Blur alphabet 'A'

3. Put the entire number in a green circle.

That's it, just by doing this simple remedy, you can easily tackle the wrong house number.

MAY I ASK YOU FOR A SMALL FAVOR?

I want to express my sincere gratitude for choosing to invest your time in reading this book. Your decision to explore this work among countless others means a lot to me.

I hope that within these pages, you've discovered actionable insights that can enhance your daily life. Your journey doesn't have to end here, though.

May I kindly request an additional 30 seconds of your valuable time?

Sharing your thoughts about the book through a review would be immensely appreciated. Your review serves as a beacon, guiding other readers to take a chance on my books. It's a small gesture that carries significant weight in the world of authors.

To submit your review effortlessly, please scan the below **QR Code**. It will take you directly to the book's review page:

"Master Your MONEY With Numerology"

Alternatively, you can also find the "**Reviews Section**" of this book's page on Amazon.

Your review will require just a minute of your time but will make a monumental difference in helping me connect with a broader audience and I eagerly look forward to reading your review.

Once again, thank you for your unwavering support of my work.

CHAPTER 7

HOME SWEET GOALS: WHEN AND HOW YOU'LL OWN?

*"Numerology is the key to the secrets of the universe." - **Pythagoras***

M any people live in rented houses, and they ask me when they will get their own house. In this chapter, we will discuss what problems are stopping you from getting your own house and how you can fix those problems.

First of all, write your date of birth on paper and find your driver and conductor number. For example, my date of birth is 02 May 1991 and my driver number is 2 and my conductor is 9.

Look into your birth date, month, and year, and into your driver and conductor. Do you have numbers 2, 5, and 8?

If all three numbers are absent or only one of them is present, there are very low chances that you will get your own house.

First of all, we need to fulfill the requirement of these numbers. Numbers 2,5,8 are the numbers of the Moon, Mercury, and Saturn. These numbers are called **Earth Elements**.

You should wear a crystal bracelet on your left hand or you can wear a garland made up of crystal. Crystal improves Earth's elements and increases the chances of owning a house.

Do one more thing: walk barefoot daily for at least 30 minutes. You can walk anywhere and anytime within 24 hours. You can walk inside your house, on the rooftop, or on the grass in a garden. When you walk barefoot, basically you are walking directly on the earth. This method will transfer the power of the earth in your body through your feet and will fulfill the requirements of earth elements in your chart.

By doing these two simple remedies, you can increase the chances of owning a house. The house you were supposed to get after 10 years, you will get in just 2 years. When your house is ready. Avoid taking out a loan against that house and don't sell that house. If you do this, you will have a lot of trouble getting back to your house.

CHAPTER 8

DECODE YOUR CAR'S ENERGY: NUMEROLOGY TIPS AND REMEDIES

*"Prosperity is not just about dollars and cents; it's about aligning your financial choices with the rhythm of the universe. Master Your MONEY With Numerology unveils the cosmic dance of abundance." – **Sooraj Achar***

I f you are going to purchase a car, how will you calculate the car's number? Let's find out in this chapter.

Suppose the car number is: DL 3C AB 1234. It is an alphanumeric number associated with the respective RTO where the car is registered. The first 6 letters, 'DL 3C AB,' represent the series, and it will be the same for 9999 cars. The formula remains the same; we will not calculate static numbers, so our focus will be only on the last four digits, 1234.

The numerological number of this car will be 1+2+3+4 = 10, which further simplifies to 1+0 = 1.

Now that you have the numerological number of your car, you can easily compare this number with your DOB to see if it is compatible with you or not. For example, if the car number is 1 and your driver is 8, you should not buy the car, as the numbers are not compatible.

When you purchase a new car, the system assigns the car number; it's not in your hands to choose a car number of your preference. However, you can pay a little extra to get a number of your choice. If you don't want to pay extra for a specific number, you can place a car protection pyramid on the dashboard of your car.

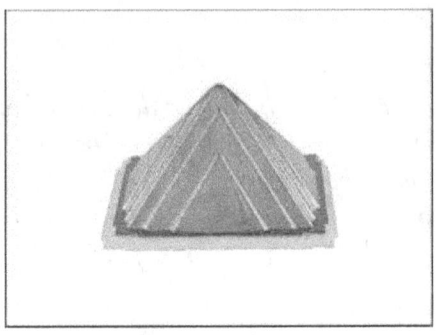

If possible choose a number in which digits are in ascending order (left to right), i.e. 1234, 3579, 0368, 0339, etc. This will be icing on the cake but don't forget to match the number with your DOB.

CHAPTER 9

SELL YOUR UNSOLD PROPERTIES USING NUMEROLOGY

"Numerology is the study of the universal language of numbers and how they can be used to understand the hidden truths of the universe."
- Dr. Richard Craze

In this chapter, we will talk about how you can fix the problems/ troubles in selling out a property. If you have a property (i.e. residential, commercial, flat fully furnished house, or a plot) and you are facing issues selling out that property. I will tell you two methods. Both of them are very important to you. Both methods complement each other.

First of all, grab the papers of your property and place them in the northwest zone of your property. If the Northwest zone is not available, you can place them in the West direction. If both

39

zones are occupied or not available, you can place the papers in the north direction. Make sure your papers should not be in the South-west or South zone. Maybe you are getting many customers to see your property, but you are still not able to make a deal. The position of your property's peppers may be the cause of not getting the deal.

If your papers are in a bank, you can still follow the same process with the photocopies of the original papers. This is as good as your original papers.

Now the second method.

Do you have a window or balcony in the Northwest zone of the house you are currently living in? If yes! This will work as a catalyst for selling out your property. Bring two wind chimes from the market in yellow or golden tones. One wind charm must have five rods and the other one must have six rods. At least one rod of both wind chimes must be a length of 11 inches. Hang these wind chimes in that window of the balcony. The distance between them should be about 1 meter. The sound of these wind chimes will activate your Northwest zone. This is called **Sound Therapy**. This sound will knock on the door of your universe and send your message to your universe. It connects the energy between you and your universe and removes the obstacles in the way.

If you don't have a window or balcony, don't make the mistake of hanging them inside your house. If you hang them indoors, they cannot be activated by wind energy and there is no use if they are not getting activated. They can even create noise or sound pollution by the waves of your fan if you hang them inside your house.

By following these two remedies, you will get a perfect deal.

CHAPTER 10

KARMIC DEBTS OF PREVIOUS BIRTH !!

"Money is energy, and numbers are its language. Let Master Your MONEY With Numerology be your translator, guiding you to speak the language of financial abundance."
- Sooraj Achar

Karmic numbers mean Karmic debts. When someone is born in karmic numbers, it is believed that they are carrying debts from their previous life to this life. If they do not clear the debts in this life, they have to carry them forward into their next life. They are carrying these debts because they made some mistakes and sins in their past lives.

First of all, let's see what the karmic numbers are:

10, 13, 14, 16, and 19 are the karmic numbers. If someone is born on these dates in any month, it is said that they are ruled by a Karmic number.

God says what you have done in your previous life, most probably, you will do the same in this life. So good will provide you with the same atmosphere as your previous life. You will be given the same powers as in your previous life. God will observe if you are misusing your power if you are misusing your freedom, if you are misusing the environment and authority or not. If you misuse your life, you will be born again into a karmic number in your next life.

Let's study each Karmic Number:

1. Karmic Number 10:

People with the karmic number 10 have a clean slate. A clean slate means they have no previous debts, but they haven't done any positive deeds in their past life. According to their deeds in this life, God will decide whether they will go into a karmic number or not in the next life. 10 is not as karmic as other numbers are. If you are ruled by the number 10, you should try to do more and more good and positive deeds for society. You can avoid your next karmic birth by doing all of these things.

2. Karmic Number 13:

This number is called "**All work and no play**".

This person must have committed many sins and bad deeds in his past life. Maybe he was a gangster because this is the number of Rahu. Maybe he was a thief or a robber. Maybe he was a murderer.

These people will have to do much more hard work. If you are born into this number, you have to do much more hard work to get anything compared to others. You should avoid any bad deeds and try to do positive deeds so that you can please God.

3. Karmic Number 14:

The tagline for this number is **"Abuse of Freedom"**.

These people must have abused their freedom in their past lives. Maybe they were someone's cashier or someone's manager, and they might have misappropriated someone's money. They might have committed money-related fraud in the past life. If they continue to abuse their freedom in this life, they have to give birth again in a karmic number in their next life.

4. Karmic Number 16:

This number is "**Abuse of Love**". They must have abused their love in their past lives. Maybe they were involved in extramarital affairs. If they do the same in this life, they have to face many problems like disturbed married life and divorce, and if they continue all these things in this life, they will be born in a karmic number again in their next life. These people should try to be loyal to their loved ones.

5. Karmic Number 19:

This number is "**Abuse of Power**".

They must have misused their power in their past life. Maybe they were a prime minister, a chief minister, or in a powerful post in their past life. They might have exploited people with their power.

In this life, they will be given powers and authority again. If they misuse this again, they will be born in karmic numbers again.

If you are born with a karmic number, there is only one way to get rid of it: Good Deeds and Good Karma.

Through good deeds, you can wipe away all the sins and mistakes of your past life. You can reduce your burden and you can clean your slate.

CHAPTER 11

NUMEROLOGY FOR STOCK MARKET

*"In the symphony of financial success, each number plays a unique melody. Learn the harmonies of wealth with Master Your MONEY With Numerology and compose your financial masterpiece." – **Sooraj Achar***

Everyone thinks about investing in the stock market. Should you play in the stock market? Is the stock market lucky or unlucky for you? Let's know about all these probabilities according to numerology.

Numbers of the stock market:

1. **6**: Because it is the number of Venus, it is the number of money and luxuries. You can play with the stocks if 6 is in your DOB. If 6 is not present in your DOB it gives a weak indication towards the stock market.

2. **5**: this is the number of Mercury and a balancing number. This number is good for investing in stocks.

If both 5 and 6 are in your date of birth (DOB), it is a very good indication. You can consider making changes in the stock market. There is a high probability of achieving high returns. However, remember that there are also many other factors present in our DOB that can affect the success rate. Therefore, we must carefully examine our DOB before taking any chances in the stock market.

Let's understand with an example:

Assume a date of birth is 17-06-1985 with the presence of 5 & 6 and this is the chart-

D=8

C=1

In this date of birth, the birth driver and conductor are anti-numbers, and the driver itself is a struggling number. Number 8 can bring financial gains, but it often requires significant effort and hard work. In contrast, the stock market is often seen as a source of relatively easy money. Therefore, the stock market may not be a suitable match for individuals with the driver number 8.

Even though numbers 5 and 6 are both there in the DOB but, the driver is always the dominating factor therefore this person should keep distance from the stock market.

Let's take one more example;

Assume a DOB is 12-06-1985 and the chart is-

D=3

C=5

You can see that both 5 and 6 are there in this DOB but the problem here is with the driver 3. Which is the number of Jupiter, the number of education, wisdom, healing, and health sectors. In this can the driver is not comfortable with the stock market.

Let's take one more example:

Assume a dob is 15-05-1983 and here is the chart-

D=6

C=5

This date of birth is perfect for the stock market. Because there is 5 in the chart and the driver number is the number of Venus.

There are some more probabilities for the stock market:

1. D= 1, and 6 is present. This is favorable for the stock market. But the conductor cannot be 8.

2. D=2, and 6 is present. This is favorable for the stock market.

3. D=3, not favorable.

4. D=4, not favorable.

5. D=5, favorable.

6. D=6, best favorable condition.

7. D=7 can take a chance.

8. D=8, not favorable

9. D=9, not favorable.

Remember that we also need to check if the D-C combination is not anti or opposite and it is not preferable to invest in the stock market if number 6 is missing.

Investing Without Having 5 & 6:

Suppose a DOB is 21-7-1983, the chart will be:

D= 3

C= 4

You can see that both 5 and 6 are absent in this DOB and chart. However, this person can enter the stock market with a high chance of success. They can potentially become the king of the stock market, but they should enter differently, like a wild card entry. This individual should refrain from investing their own money directly into stocks or engaging in trading; instead, they can become a broker and offer investment consultancy services. But what's the reason behind this?

To operate a brokerage and consultancy business, you require knowledge, wisdom, and very accurate intuition. The presence of 3 and 7 works in favor of this. Additionally, the presence of 2 alongside 7 gives a sixth sense to the person.

If these factors are present in your date of birth, you can earn money from the stock market, not as an investor or trader, but as a broker or consultant.

This was all about the stock market and the numerology behind it. Remember even though we have many factors in our favor stock market is a very risky place so trade wisely.

CHAPTER 12

TOP-5 TIPS & TRICKS IN NUMEROLOGY

"No," said Hermione shortly. "Have either of you seen my copy of Numerology and Gramatica?" Oh, yeah, I borrowed it for a bit of bedtime reading." said Ron, but very quietly."
- J. K. Rowling

Trick Number 1:

Without knowing someone's date of birth, you can tell which numbers are absent from their date of birth.

If there is a male or female and they are not wearing a watch/ wearing a leather or rubber strap watch. You can definitely say that the number 6 or 7 or both numbers are absent from their date of birth.

Because number 7 is the number of silver metal and number 6 is the metal of gold metal.

If you give them a metal strap watch first, they will refuse to wear it. If they wear it they can lose it, or they can get an allergy from it.

If they are wearing only a silver-colored watch, you can say that the number 6 may be absent, but 7 is present on their date of birth.

This formula applies to 70 to 75% of people.

Trick Number 2:

By using this trick, you can tell someone about their broken affairs, multiple affairs, or extramarital affairs. This formula applies to 70 to 80% of people, no matter whether they are male or female.

If someone has multiple sevens (more than one) in their chart. There are high chances of broken affairs, multiple affairs, and extramarital affairs. As the quantity of 7s increases, these chances also increase.

Trick Number 3:

By this trick, you tell someone that they have money in every pocket of their dress/suit. They have money in each drawer of their almirah; they have multiple bank accounts, and there is money under their pillow and bed.

This formula is applicable to people with multiple 8s (more than one) in their chart. This formula is applicable. As the number of 8s increases, chances also increase. This is applicable to 70 to 75% of people.

Trick Number 4:

By this trick, you can identify a person with a good 6th sense.

If 2 and 7 both numbers are present and on their birth chart, they have an extremely good 6th sense.

If multiple 2s and multiple 7s are present, their 6th sense is on another level.

These are the people who can predict correctly. Before leaving their house, they already know that their vehicle can get punctured, they can predict rainfall, and they already know that someone is going to cheat them. Their intuition power is very strong.

Trick Number 5:

You can predict the person who always lives around priests, numerologists, and astrologers. You can predict a person who visits temples, religious sites, and pilgrimage frequently.

It happens when number 3 (Jupiter) and number 7 (Ketu) are present in someone's chart.

If these numbers are present multiple times, chances increase.

These tricks are not applicable to 100% of people because there are other factors, but these tricks are applicable to 70 to 75% of people. You can mesmerize anyone with these tricks.

CHAPTER HIGHLIGHTS: TOP 5 TAKEAWAYS AND INSIGHTS

1. Key Takeaways for the Chapter - How To Detect Money Sector?

1. Discovering Your Fortunes: Your date of birth holds three significant lotteries – the Driver No., Conductor No., and Kua No. These lotteries act as powerful forces that can shape your destiny.

2. Understanding the Driver No. Lottery: If your Driver No. is absent in your date of birth, it's like hitting the jackpot. This absence indicates a lottery, bringing unexpected and transformative energy to your life.

3. Exploring Conductor No. Lottery: If your Conductor No. is already present in your date of birth, it means you don't have the Conductor lottery. However, its absence could signify another lottery, enhancing the potential for positive change.

4. Unveiling the Kua No. Lottery: Similar to the Conductor lottery, the absence of your Kua No. in your date of birth hints at another lottery. This lottery can bring forth unique opportunities and advantages in your life.

5. Powerful Jackpots: If a lottery number completes a line in your birth chart, it transforms from a mere lottery to a powerful jackpot. These completed lines indicate a convergence of favorable energies, promising significant success and prosperity.

Embark on a journey of self-discovery as you unravel the lotteries hidden within your date of birth. Each absence could be the key to unlocking unforeseen opportunities and shaping a future filled with abundance and success.

2. Key Takeaways for the Chapter - Common Factor Among Rich & Successful People

1. Key Success Factor: 9-5-1 - The common factor for success among the richest individuals is the presence of 9-5-1 in their date of birth (DOB). Identifying this combination in your DOB can unlock your potential for significant success.

2. Destined for Success - If your DOB includes the numbers 9, 5, and 1, it suggests a predisposition for success. This combination signifies power, balance, wisdom, and the spirit of a leader.

3. Exemplary Figures - Examining the DOBs of successful individuals like Jeff Bezos, Mukesh Ambani, Ratan Tata, and Bollywood icons reveals the presence of 9-5-1. This commonality aligns with their remarkable achievements.

4. Numerical Significance - Number 9 represents power, 5 brings balance and wisdom, and 1 symbolizes leadership. The combination creates a potent force for success, reflecting qualities of strength, knowledge, and kingly attributes.

5. Intention and Clarity - While possessing 9-5-1 is advantageous, success also hinges on good intentions and clear goals. Ensuring positive intent and focused objectives enhances the likelihood of realizing the inherent potential in these numbers.

3. Key Takeaways for the Chapter - Power Of Number 6: Venus

1. Era of Venus Wealth: In the Venusian era of wealth and luxury, this chapter explores methods to uplift the planet Venus, associated with the number 6 and the color white.

2. Numerical Associations: If Venus is significant in your birth chart or your driver/conductor is 6, follow remedies. However, caution against a driver or conductor with the number 3, as it opposes Venus.

3. Remedies for Venus Upliftment: Donate white items on Fridays to the needy, wear white, or keep white objects. Temple donations are an option if reaching the needy is challenging.

4. Precaution Against Jupiter: If Venus is influential, avoid the color yellow, linked to Jupiter, Venus's antagonist.

5. Cosmic Harmony: Embracing Venus's energy aligns with cosmic forces, inviting prosperity. By adopting remedies and precautions, one can uplift Venusian aspects for a life adorned with abundance and grace.

4. Key Takeaways for the Chapter - Unlocking The Future: Predictions Beyond The Date Of Birth

1. Numerology's Essence: Numerology delves into the power and significance of numbers, unraveling their influence on our lives. Dr. Michael Losier emphasizes its role in understanding the profound meanings behind numbers.

2. Dealing with Unknown Birthdates: Explore a unique tool for predicting life events when individuals are unaware of their birth details. Discover how to navigate uncertainties, providing insights even when the date of birth is unknown.

3. The Pyramid Method: Learn a hypothetical example using the Pyramid of Numbers. When faced with a client's question, transform the words into numerical values, creating a single-digit number through the Pyramid Method.

4. Interpreting the Result: Understand the correlation between the derived number and the answer. Utilize a handy table to interpret whether the outcome is a "yes" or "no." This method offers a simple yet effective way to provide guidance without precise birth information.

5. Answering Life's Queries: Master the art of answering questions related to various aspects of life, offering predictions with numerical precision. Uncover the mysteries of the Pyramid Numerology technique to navigate uncertainties and provide meaningful insights.

5. Key Takeaways for the Chapter - Jackpot: Big Arrows And Small Arrows

1. Numeric Architects of Wealth: Explore the profound influence of numbers as the silent architects of financial destinies. Sooraj Achar's guide unveils the numerical language of wealth, providing insights into the subtle codes shaping prosperity.

2. Loshu Grid Insights: Delve into the intricacies of the Loshu Grid, discovering the significance of lines and arrows. These symbols, derived from the grid, offer valuable insights into an individual's traits, capabilities, and inclinations.

3. Big Arrows - Vertical Insights: Uncover the Planner Arrow (4, 3, 8) for strategic planners, the Decision-Maker Arrow (9, 5, 1) for fighters, and the Opportunity-Grabber Arrow (2, 7, 6) for those excelling in sports and seizing chances.

4. Big Arrows - Horizontal Revelations: Decode the Sharp Memory Arrow (4, 9, 2), the Golden Heart Arrow (3, 5, 7) for compassionate individuals, and the Prosperity Arrow (8, 1, 6) symbolizing practical prosperity.

5. Diagonal Arrows and Small Arrows: Understand the Aggressive and Balanced Arrow (4, 5, 6), the Patient and Goal-oriented Arrow (2, 5, 8), and small arrows like the Balance in Difficult Situations, Deep Research, Spiritual and Knowledgeable, and the Arrow of Litigation and Argumentation.

Bonus: Gain a deeper understanding of how these arrows shape personalities, guiding individuals toward financial success and personal fulfillment.

6. Key Takeaways for the Chapter - A Guide To House Numbers And Remedial Measures

1. Alphabets in House Numbers: Decode the influence of alphabets in house numbers. For house numbers like A/512, understand that the alphabet 'A' is static, and only the numerical part contributes to the house's energy. Calculate the numerical value (e.g., 5+1+2) for insights into the house's vibrations.

2. Alphabets at the End: Explore cases where alphabets are at the end of house numbers (e.g., 512A). Recognize that in this scenario, both the number and alphabet contribute to the house's energy. Calculate the value of the alphabet as well (e.g., 5+1+2+1), ensuring a comprehensive understanding of the house's numeric resonance.

3. Handling '/' in House Numbers: Address confusion arising from house numbers with '/'. Learn to distinguish between static block numbers and variable house numbers. Utilize information from adjacent houses to identify which part of the number is static and which is changing, ensuring accurate numerology calculations.

4. Tower Numbers: Simplify calculations for tower numbers. If your house is in tower 2 and the flat number is 409, focus on the variable part (4+0+9) for numerology insights. Tower numbers, being static, don't impact the calculation, streamlining the process.

5. Remedies for Wrong House Numbers: Recognize wrong house numbers that may conflict with numerology principles. Implement remedies such as using symbols like '-' or '/', blurring alphabets, and enclosing the entire number in a green circle to mitigate negative effects and harmonize the energy of the house.

Bonus: Gain practical insights into ensuring your home's numerology aligns with your personal vibrations, fostering a harmonious living space conducive to financial well-being.

7. Key Takeaways for the Chapter - Home Sweet Goals: When And How You'll Own?

1. Numerological Analysis: Decode the numerology of your date of birth to unveil your driver and conductor numbers. Focus on numbers 2, 5, and 8, associated with the Moon, Mercury, and Saturn, as they are crucial for home ownership. Assess if these numbers are present in your birth details.

2. Identifying Obstacles: Recognize obstacles hindering your path to homeownership. If numbers 2, 5, and 8 are absent or only one is present, understand that the chances of owning a house are significantly reduced. Addressing this absence becomes the first step toward achieving your dream home.

3. Earth Elements Enhancement: Boost the influence of Earth elements (2, 5, 8) by wearing a crystal bracelet on your left hand. Alternatively, a crystal garland can serve the purpose. Enhancing these elements aligns your energy with the vibrations conducive to owning a house.

4. Barefoot Walking Ritual: Incorporate a simple yet powerful remedy by walking barefoot for at least 30 minutes daily. This practice connects you directly to the Earth, transferring its energy through your feet. Fulfilling the Earth element requirements in your chart, this ritual accelerates the manifestation of your homeownership aspirations.

5. Timely Results and Caution: Experience accelerated results, potentially turning a 10-year wait into just 2 years for your dream house. Once you achieve homeownership, avoid taking loans against the property and refrain from selling it to prevent complications and secure the stability of your newfound residence.

8. Key Takeaways for the Chapter - Decode Your Car's Energy: Numerology Tips And Remedies

1. Car Number Calculation: Learn the art of calculating the numerological number for your car using its registration digits. Focus on the last four digits, such as DL 3C AB 1234, with the numerological sum derived from 1+2+3+4, simplifying to 1. This number represents the cosmic energy associated with your vehicle.

2. Compatibility Check: Assess the compatibility between your car's numerological number and your date of birth (DOB). If the numbers align positively, it enhances harmony and connection between you and your vehicle. Avoid purchasing a car if the numbers clash, ensuring a better energetic resonance.

3. Numerology and Car Choice: Understand that the system usually assigns car numbers, but you can opt for a specific

number by paying extra. Prioritize choosing numbers in ascending order (e.g., 1234, 3579) for added positivity. However, always cross-reference with your DOB for optimal vibrational alignment.

4. Personalized Car Protection Pyramid: Enhance the positive energy in your car by placing a car protection pyramid on the dashboard. This simple yet effective remedy helps harmonize the cosmic vibrations within your vehicle, contributing to a smoother and more prosperous journey.

5. Ascending Order Preference: Consider selecting a car number with digits in ascending order for an additional energetic boost. Examples include 1234, 3579, 0368, 0339, etc. While this is an extra touch, prioritize compatibility with your DOB to ensure a favorable and aligned connection with your vehicle.

9. Key Takeaways for the Chapter - Sell Your Unsold Properties Using Numerology

1. Zone Placement: Locate property papers in the northwest or west zone, avoiding south areas. Photocopies work if the originals are with the bank.

2. Sound Therapy: Hang yellow or golden wind chimes with 5 and 6 rods in the northwest window or balcony for sound activation. Maintain a 1-meter distance. Avoid indoor placement for effective wind energy activation.

3. Catalyst for Sale: Combined methods enhance energy flow, acting as a catalyst for selling the property.

4. Obstacle Removal: Sound therapy connects with the universe, removing obstacles and facilitating a perfect deal.

5. Strategic Placement: Attention to zone details and wind chime positioning optimizes the effectiveness of remedies.

10. Key Takeaways for the Chapter - Karmic Debts Of Previous Birth !!

1. Karmic Debt Concept: Karmic numbers (10, 13, 14, 16, 19) signify debts carried from past lives, reflecting past actions and deeds.

2. Karmic Number 10: Clean slate individuals with an opportunity to shape their destiny through positive deeds, potentially avoiding karmic births.

3. Karmic Number 13: Symbolizes hard work and potential past involvement in negative activities. Encourages diligent efforts to counterbalance past deeds.

4. Karmic Number 14: Represents the abuse of freedom and potential involvement in fraudulent activities. Urges individuals to avoid repeating mistakes.

5. Karmic Numbers 16 and 19: Signify the abuse of love and power, respectively. Individuals must remain loyal in relationships and use authority responsibly to avoid recurring karmic cycles.

6. Redemption Through Good Deeds: The key to breaking free from karmic numbers lies in committing to positive actions, wiping away past sins, and reducing the burden for a clean slate in future lives.

11. Key Takeaways for the Chapter - Numerology For Stock Market

1. Numerological Analysis for Stock Market: Understand the influence of specific numbers in your date of birth (DOB) on stock market endeavors. The presence or absence of numbers like 5 and 6 plays a crucial role in determining compatibility with stock market activities.

2. Impact of Individual Numbers: Evaluate the significance of individual numbers in the DOB for stock market involvement. For example, the number 6 (Venus) is favorable, while number 8 may pose challenges. Consider the dominating influence of the driver number in decision-making.

3. Driver-Conductor Compatibility: Ensure compatibility between the driver and conductor numbers. An anti or opposite combination may indicate unfavorable conditions for stock market ventures. For instance, the presence of 5 and 6 is beneficial, but the conductor cannot be 8.

4. Exceptions and Strategies: Explore exceptions where individuals lacking 5 and 6 in their DOB can still succeed in the stock market. Such individuals can consider alternative roles like becoming brokers or consultants, leveraging their wisdom, knowledge, and intuition.

5. Risk and Caution: Acknowledge the inherent risks in the stock market and exercise caution. While numerology provides insights, prudent decision-making, and strategic trading are essential for success. Approach stock market involvement with wisdom and consider the broader context of your DOB.

12. Key Takeaways for the Chapter - Top-5 Tips & Tricks In Numerology

1. Identifying Absent Numbers: Without knowing the birth date, observe a person's choice of watch strap. A leather or rubber strap signals the absence of numbers 6 or 7, while a silver-colored watch may indicate the presence of 7.

2. Affairs Prediction: Multiple sevens in a person's chart suggest a higher likelihood of broken, multiple, or extramarital affairs. The more sevens, the greater the chances, applicable to 70-80% of individuals.

3. Wealth Indicators: Spot indications of wealth distribution by observing multiple eights in a person's chart. The presence of multiple eights suggests money in various pockets, drawers, and accounts, applicable to 70-75% of people.

4. Enhanced 6th Sense: The presence of both 2 and 7 in a birth chart signifies a strong 6th sense. Multiple instances of these numbers indicate an exceptionally heightened intuition, enabling accurate predictions.

5. Religious Inclinations: Identifying individuals who frequent priests, numerologists, and temples are possible with the presence of numbers 3 (Jupiter) and 7 (Ketu). Multiple occurrences enhance the likelihood, offering insights into a person's spiritual tendencies.

CONCLUSION

Congratulations on reaching the culmination of this book. Your commitment to reading through these pages signifies your dedication to personal growth and a thirst for knowledge. Completing a book is a remarkable achievement, and you should take a moment to acknowledge your accomplishment.

Throughout this journey, the aim has been to guide you toward shaping a destiny defined by success and fulfillment. Your investment in this book reflects a deep commitment to self-improvement, and for that, you should feel proud.

As you conclude this book, I trust that it has left you with valuable insights and a sense of empowerment. The road to a prosperous destiny is not always linear or without its challenges, but your newfound knowledge in smart questioning equips you to navigate these paths with confidence.

I genuinely hope that your voyage through these chapters has been both enlightening and engaging. The pursuit of a splendid life brimming with happiness and fulfillment is a commendable one, and your proactive steps toward this aspiration are evident through your persistence in reading this book.

In the pursuit of success and a life well-lived, remember that knowledge is your most potent tool. With this, you hold the key to unlocking the limitless potential within you.

As you close this final page and embark on the journey that follows, I extend my heartfelt best wishes for a future filled with accomplishments and contentment.

Cheers,
Sooraj Achar

MAY I ASK YOU FOR A SMALL FAVOR?

I want to express my sincere gratitude for choosing to invest your time in reading this book. Your decision to explore this work among countless others means a lot to me.

I hope that within these pages, you've discovered actionable insights that can enhance your daily life. Your journey doesn't have to end here, though.

May I kindly request an additional 30 seconds of your valuable time?

Sharing your thoughts about the book through a review would be immensely appreciated. Your review serves as a beacon, guiding other readers to take a chance on my books. It's a small gesture that carries significant weight in the world of authors.

To submit your review effortlessly, please scan the below **QR Code**. It will take you directly to the book's review page:

"Master Your MONEY With Numerology"

Alternatively, you can also find the "**Reviews Section**" of this book's page on Amazon.

Your review will require just a minute of your time but will make a monumental difference in helping me connect with a broader audience and I eagerly look forward to reading your review.

Once again, thank you for your unwavering support of my work.

DO YOU WANT ME TO PERSONALLY HELP?

BOOK A FREE 30-MINUTE NUMEROLOGY CONSULTATION

You're invited to book a **free 30-minute one-on-one consultation** with renowned Numerology and Vastu Coach and Consultant, Sooraj Achar. This personalized session will help you understand your Numerology birth chart and reveal your strengths, weaknesses, and more. Also get an opportunity to apply for your Detailed Numerology Fortune Report.

Topics Covered in Your Detailed Numerology Fortune Report:

1. Detailed Characteristics

2. What Your Driver-Conductor Combination Says About You

3. Insights from the Yogas in Your DOB

4. Detailed Birth Chart Analysis

5. How to Craft Your Signature

6. Lucky and Unlucky Numbers

7. Neutral Numbers

8. Lucky and Unlucky Colors

9. Designing Your Business Card

10. Relationship Insights

11. Impact of Repetitive Numbers in Your DOB

12. Influence of Missing Numbers in Your DOB

13. Remedies for Missing Numbers

14. Predictions for the Next 5 Years

15. Name Number Compatibility

16. Name Spelling Corrections

17. Mobile Number Compatibility

18. Professional Life Guidance

19. Yantra/Pendant Remedies

20. Health Sector Analysis

Free Bonuses:

- 10 **Numerology Books Bundle**, covering 100+ unique topics

- 2 **Free 1-2-1 Consultations**

"Free 30-Minute Numerology Consultation"

Ready to Talk? Click the Link Above or Scan the **QR Code** Below to Book a Free Call

Don't miss this opportunity to gain profound insights into your life. Book your free consultation today and claim your detailed Numerology report.

PREVIEW OF MY NEXT BOOK IN THE SERIES

Master Your PROFESSIONAL GOALS With Numerology

This book is **Numerology Professional Success Guide**, where you get to learn the advanced level of numerology application and implementation to transform your life towards a happier destiny.

Below is the list of **Important Topics** to be Covered in the **Upcoming Books** in the **Numerology Series**:

1. Choosing The Right Profession

2. How To Detect Job Or Business

3. Foreign Opportunities Or Abroad Settlement

4. Professions According To Yogas

5. Profession Of Anti & Opposite D-C Combination

6. Is Your Child Weak In Studies?

7. How To Detect Education Sector

8. Trying Hard To Get A Government Job?

9. Who Can Be A Coach And Player

10. Visiting/Business Card Design

Stay Tuned to explore all the series of **Self-Help** Books coming up !!

PREVIEW OF MY BEST SELLING BOOKS

<u>Series-1</u>: <u>Master Your Life with</u>
<u>NUMEROLOGY</u>

❑ **Why do 80% of People Fail to Recognize their True Potential ??**

These self-help books will help you **Recognize, Transform, and Navigate** your life toward a **Happier Destiny**.

I always say that your **Date of Birth** is so precious. God has placed many diamonds on your date of birth that you are not aware of. It doesn't matter if your date of birth is good or bad. The idea is how you can take the best out of your date of birth. **Master Your DESTINY With Numerology** is a perfect, **complete beginner's guide** for those who are new to numerology.

❑ **What Role Does Numerology Play in Your Life?**

- You have been surrounded by numbers since the

day you were Born. Now use them to unlock your Destiny.

- Wherever you go in your life, the numbers always move on with you.

- When you are born, on the very first day of your life, you get your date of birth, which is made up of numbers.

- When you get admitted to school, you get your roll number.

- When you get your results, you get a percentage of numbers.

- When you get a job, you get a salary and EMP-ID number.

- When you buy any vehicle, it has a number plate.

- When you travel, you get a ticket and seat number

- When you check into a hotel, you get a room number.

- When you want to call a person, you have to dial numbers.

- When you get married, there is also a date attached to it.

- If there is Life, there are Numbers. You cannot get rid of Numbers.

◻ Your **Name Spelling** also plays an important role according to your date of birth. Believe me or not, **30% to 40%** of your success or failure depends on your name spelling. If you keep your name spelling correct, you can achieve 30% to 40% more success in your life.

◻ **Master Your DESTINY With Numerology will help you...**

◻ Recognize Your Strengths and Weaknesses.

◻ Find Your Lucky Numbers and Colors.

◻ Correct Your Name Spelling without changing your documents.

◻ Choose the Right Profession.

◻ Find a Compatible Life-Partner.

◻ With Simple Remedies for All Your Problems.

◻ Check Your Foreign or Abroad Opportunities.

◻ Predict your Future Years, Months, and Days of importance, which helps you make Better Decisions.

◻ Understand the Behavioral Patterns of People Around You.

◻ Transform and Navigate your life for a Better Future.

◻ If you are ready to make a commitment to yourself that you want to learn everything that is presented to you, then it is our commitment to you that this will surely help you a lot. There is no reason why this book will not change your destiny or transform your future. But, there is an important thing you must keep in mind, i.e., **"You will bring this change through TRANSFORMATION, not through MIRACLES".**

☐ If you learn **Numerology**, then

(a) "You will be **awakened**", which makes it likely to "**transform**" your life.

(b) Ultimately, "You will be able to **navigate** your life".

☐ Life is all about **"Awakening,"**, **"Transformation,"** and eventually, "Knowing How To **Navigate** It?"

☐ Order **Master Your DESTINY With Numerology** now to make the most of your **Health, Relationships, Career, and Money** by unlocking the **Power of Numbers**.

<u>Check Out My Best Selling Books Here:</u>

 **1. Master Your DESTINY With Numerology**

 **2. Master Your NAME-SPELLING With Numerology**

 **3. Master Your RELATIONSHIPS With Numerology**

 **4. Master Your MONEY With Numerology**

5. Master Your HEALTH With Numerology

6. Master Your PROFESSIONAL GOALS With Numerology

Series-2: Master Your Life with VASTU

❑ **How Can These Books Work Miracles in Your Life?**

This Self-Help Book is A Perfect Blueprint Describing Ancient Principles for Modern Living. A Step-by-step Practical Guide for Beginners to Creating a Positive Living Space and for Optimal Well-Being.

Learn:

❑ **How to Implement Feng-Shui/Vastu in your Day-to-Day Life !!**

❑ **What Role Do Feng-Shui and Vastu Play in Your Life?**

❑ **Relationship between Vastu and Feng-Shui?**

Vastu is used to Diagnose, and Feng Shui is the Remedy. Vastu is used to identify the disease, and Feng Shui is the medicine. Vastu and Feng Shui are complementary to each other.

Vastu Shastra is an Ancient Indian Science of architecture and construction, which is based on the principles of harmony and balance between humans and their environment. The main focus of Vastu is to create a harmonious balance between the 5-Elements of nature, i.e., Earth, Water, Air, Fire, & Space. It emphasizes directions and orientation and uses various elements like colors, shapes, and materials to create a balance and positive energy in the living spaces.

Feng Shui, on the other hand, is a Chinese Philosophical System of harmonizing everyone with the surrounding environment. It is based on the principles of Qi (Chi), the life force that flows through all living things, and Yin and Yang, the balance of opposite forces. Feng Shui focuses on the placement of objects, furniture, and structures in living spaces to optimize the flow of energy, or "Qi." It also considers the orientation of the building, the placement of doors and windows, and the use of colors, shapes, & materials to create balance & harmony.

In summary, both Vastu and Feng Shui aim to create balance and harmony in living spaces, but Vastu is more focused on directions and orientation, while Feng Shui emphasizes the flow of energy & balance of opposing forces.

◻ The Benefits of Reading This Book Include:

◻ **Health and Well-Being:** Vastu principles aim to create a harmonious and balanced environment that can promote physical, mental, and emotional well-being.

◻ **Financial Prosperity:** Vastu principles are believed to help attract positive energy and good fortune, leading to financial prosperity.

◻ **Improved Relationships:** Vastu principles can help create an atmosphere of peace and harmony, which can lead to improved relationships with family, friends, & colleagues.

◻ **Increased Productivity:** A Vastu-compliant environment is said to be conducive to productivity and efficiency, leading to greater success in personal & professional life.

◻ **Spiritual Growth:** Vastu principles are based on ancient Vedic knowledge and aim to promote spiritual growth & enlightenment.

◻ **Enhanced Creativity:** Vastu principles are believed to enhance creativity and inspiration, which can be beneficial for artists, writers, & other creative professionals.

◻ **Better Sleep Quality:** Vastu principles can help create a peaceful and relaxing environment, which can improve the quality of sleep and help reduce stress & anxiety.

◻ **Improved Mental Clarity:** A Vastu-compliant environment is said to help clear the mind and improve mental clarity, which can be beneficial for decision-making & problem-solving.

◻ **Enhanced Career Prospects:** Vastu principles can help align one's career goals with their personal strengths and abilities, leading to greater career success & satisfaction.

◻ Overall, the benefits of Vastu can contribute to a more Balanced, Harmonious, & Fulfilling Life.

◻ Order "Master Your DESTINY With Vastu" now to make the most of your Health, Relationships, Career, & Money by unlocking the Power of Directions.

Check Out My Best Selling Books Here:

1. Master Your DESTINY With Vastu

2. Master Your HOME HARMONY With Vastu

3. Master Your WEALTH With Vastu

4. Master Your CAREER With Vastu

5. Master Your HEALTH With Vastu

6. Master Your RELATIONSHIPS With Vastu

Series-3: The Ultimate Self-Healing Mastery

Embark on a transformative expedition with 'The Ultimate Self-Healing Mastery,' a soul-stirring collection designed to illuminate the path to self-discovery, healing, and fearlessness. Each book is a profound exploration of fundamental aspects of human existence, guiding readers toward a purposeful, holistic, and fearless life.

1. Discover Your Life Purpose: Reveal Your True Calling

Uncover the secrets to a fulfilling life in 'Discover Your Life Purpose.' Illuminating the essence of your being, this book takes you on a profound journey to reveal your true calling. Master the art of purposeful living, radiate enduring joy, and align your actions with your life's deeper meaning. Through insightful practices and wisdom, you'll embark on a transformative odyssey to live a life that resonates with authenticity.

Key Themes: Life Purpose, Joyful Living, Authenticity

2. The Alchemy of Healing: Master Ancient Hawaiian Technique

In 'The Alchemy of Healing,' delve into the ancient Hawaiian wisdom that transcends time. Crush negative emotions, unravel subconscious patterns, and embark on a journey of self-healing for a holistic lifestyle. This book is a guide to harnessing the power within, using age-old techniques to restore balance, foster well-being, and tap into the alchemy that transforms challenges into opportunities for growth.

Key Themes: Ancient Healing, Emotional Wellness, Self-Healing

3. The Fear of Death: Conquer Mortality Anxiety, Live a Fearless Life

Confront the universal fear in 'The Fear of Death.' Recognize the human fears surrounding mortality, and transcend anxiety by embracing death as a natural part of life's journey. This book provides profound insights into conquering fears, living fearlessly, and understanding the deeper spiritual dimensions of existence. Gain wisdom to navigate life with courage, appreciating the transient nature of our earthly sojourn.

Key Themes: Fearlessness, Death Acceptance, Spiritual Wisdom

The Unifying Thread:

Each book in 'The Ultimate Self-Healing Mastery' is a standalone guide, yet together they form a cohesive narrative of personal growth, healing, and spiritual enlightenment. Authored by experts in their respective fields, these volumes offer a holistic approach to living—a roadmap to self-realization, emotional well-being, and a fearless embrace of life's profound mysteries.

Why Read the Trilogy?

Holistic Transformation: Embark on a journey that addresses the core aspects of your existence—purpose, healing, and fearlessness.

Expert Guidance: Benefit from the insights of experts who blend ancient wisdom with modern understanding to guide you toward a more meaningful and joyful life.

Practical Wisdom: Each book is a practical guide, filled with exercises, techniques, and profound teachings that can be applied in daily life.

Life-Altering Perspectives: Gain transformative perspectives on life purpose, healing practices, and the fear of death, allowing you to navigate challenges with resilience and grace.

Experience the synergy of purpose, healing, and fearlessness—the essence of 'The Ultimate Self-Healing Mastery.' This series is not just a collection of books; it's a transformative odyssey inviting you to explore the depths of your being and awaken to the infinite possibilities that life unfolds.

<u>Check Out My Best Selling Books Here:</u>

 **1. Discover Your Life Purpose**

 **2. The Alchemy Of Healing**

 **3. The Essence of MINDFUL LIVING**

Series-4: Energize Your Mind, Body & Soul

Embark on a transformative journey of self-discovery, inner balance, and empowered living with the 'Energize Your Life Trilogy.' This compelling series unveils profound insights and practical wisdom to help you attain holistic well-being, align with your life's purpose, and cultivate the energy needed for a harmonious and fulfilling existence.

1. The Art of Balancing YIN-YANG Energy: Discover the Secret to Energized Living

Uncover the ancient wisdom of balancing YIN-YANG energy in 'The Art of Balancing YIN-YANG Energy.' This book is your guide to attaining wholeness, finding inner equilibrium, and experiencing serenity in your everyday existence. Learn the secrets of Chinese philosophy and energy balance to lead an energized life filled with vitality and peace. Discover practices to harmonize opposing forces, fostering a sense of completeness and tranquility.

Key Themes: Energy Balance, Wholeness, Serenity

2. The 7 Energy Needs: Discover the 7 Keys to Personal Fulfillment

In 'The 7 Energy Needs,' explore the keys to personal fulfillment and emotional well-being. Align your needs with your goals, master the art of balancing vital energies, and unlock the secrets to a harmonious life. This book provides a comprehensive framework for understanding and fulfilling your core energy needs, empowering you to lead a life rich in purpose, joy, and fulfillment.

Key Themes: Personal Fulfillment, Emotional Well-Being, Harmonious Life

3. The Power of ONE QUESTION: Master the Art of Smart Questioning

Ignite your journey to greatness with 'The Power of ONE QUESTION.' This book is a game-changer, offering insights into the art of smart questioning. Revolutionize your thinking, enhance decision-making, and supercharge your life and career by asking the right questions. Uncover the transformative power of focused inquiry and learn to navigate life's complexities with clarity, purpose, and a profound sense of direction.

Key Themes: Smart Questioning, Decision-Making, Journey to Greatness

The Unifying Thread:

The 'Energize Your Mind, Soul & Body' seamlessly weaves together the threads of ancient wisdom, modern psychology, and practical strategies. Each book stands as a beacon, guiding readers toward a more balanced, purposeful, and empowered life. The trilogy is designed to be both a comprehensive roadmap and a practical toolkit for individuals seeking a holistic approach to well-being and personal development.

Why Read the Trilogy?

1. **Holistic Well-Being:** Dive into a series that addresses the various dimensions of your well-being, from energy balance and emotional fulfillment to smart questioning and decision-making.

2. **Practical Wisdom:** Each book is crafted with practical exercises, actionable insights, and transformative practices that can be integrated into your daily life.

3. **Personal Empowerment:** Gain the tools and knowledge needed to take charge of your energy, align with your purpose, and make informed decisions that propel you toward greatness.

4. **Ancient Wisdom, Modern Application:** Discover the timeless principles of ancient philosophies and see how they can be applied in the context of contemporary living.

Embark on a journey of self-mastery, inner harmony, and empowered living with the '**Energize Your Mind, Body & Soul.**' Let this series be your guide as you explore the depths of your potential and unlock the secrets to a more vibrant, purposeful, and harmonious life.

Check Out My Best Selling Books Here:

 ## 1. The Art of Balancing YIN-YANG Energy

2. The Art of Mastering FEARLESS MINDSET

3. The Art of Cultivating EMOTIONAL INTELLIGENCE

4. The 7 Energy Needs

5. The Power Of ONE Question

Series-5: Achieve Life-Mastery with the NUMEROLOGY Bundle

Discover the Ultimate Path to Success with the "Achieve Life Mastery with the Numerology Bundle"

Unlock the secrets to mastering every aspect of your life with our exclusive "2 Books in 1" Numerology Series. This comprehensive bundle series combines ancient wisdom with practical insights, offering you the keys to transforming your destiny, health, relationships, finances, and professional goals.

What's Inside:

1. Master Your DESTINY And NAME-SPELLING With Numerology: "2 Books in 1"
- Book 1: Learn how your name shapes your destiny. Uncover the hidden meanings and vibrations behind your name and harness this knowledge to steer your life towards success.
- Book 2: Dive deep into numerology and discover how numbers can reveal your life's purpose, strengths, and challenges. Master your fate with personalized strategies.

2. Master Your HEALTH And RELATIONSHIPS With Numerology: "2 Books in 1"
- Book 1: Decode the numbers that influence your health. Gain insights into maintaining physical and mental well-being by aligning your lifestyle with numerological principles.
- Book 2: Enhance your relationships by understanding the compatibility and dynamics dictated by numerology. Build stronger, more meaningful connections with loved ones.

3. Master Your Money And Professional Goals With Numerology: "2 Books in 1"

- Book 1: Achieve financial freedom by leveraging numerological insights. Learn to attract wealth, make smart investments, and manage your finances with confidence.
- Book 2: Propel your career to new heights. Discover how numerology can guide you in setting and achieving professional goals, leading to a fulfilling and prosperous career.

Why Choose the "Achieve Life Mastery with the Numerology Bundle"?

- Comprehensive Guidance: Each bundle offers dual books that provide a holistic approach to understanding and applying numerology in various aspects of life.
- Practical Applications: Easy-to-follow techniques and actionable advice tailored to your unique numerological profile.
- Transformational Benefits: From personal growth to professional success, experience the profound impact of numerology on your life journey.

Start your journey towards life mastery today. Embrace the power of numbers and unlock the potential within you with the "Achieve Life Mastery with the Numerology Bundle."

Order now and take the first step towards a brighter, more prosperous future!

1. Master Your DESTINY & NAME-SPELLING With Numerology

2. Master Your HEALTH & RELATIONSHIPS With Numerology

3. Master Your MONEY & PROFESSIONAL GOALS With Numerology

Series-6: Achieve Life Mastery with the Vastu Bundle!

Unlock the secrets to a balanced, prosperous, and fulfilling life with our exclusive "2 Books in 1" Bundle Series. Dive deep into the ancient wisdom of Vastu Shastra and transform every aspect of your life with ease and grace. This comprehensive series is your gateway to mastering destiny, career, home harmony, wealth, health, and relationships.

Why Choose the Vastu Bundle?

1. Master Your DESTINY And CAREER With Vastu: 2 Books in 1 - Life Mystery Simplified

- Discover powerful Vastu techniques to align your surroundings with your career goals.

- Unlock your potential and shape your destiny with age-old principles made simple.

2. Master Your HOME HARMONY And WEALTH With Vastu: 2 Books in 1 - Life-Mystery Simplified

- Transform your home into a sanctuary of peace and prosperity.

- Attract wealth and harmony with practical Vastu tips for every corner of your home.

3. Master Your HEALTH And RELATIONSHIPS With Vastu: 2 Books in 1 - Life-Mystery Simplified

- Create a healthy living environment that nurtures your body and mind.

- Enhance your relationships and emotional well-being with Vastu insights.

Benefits of the Vastu Bundle:

- Holistic Approach: Address all key areas of life for overall well-being.

- Simplified Wisdom: Easy-to-follow guidelines, no prior knowledge needed.

- Proven Techniques: Time-tested methods for tangible results.

Transform Your Life Today!

Whether you're seeking career success, financial abundance, personal harmony, or vibrant health, the Vastu Bundle has the answers. Start your journey to life mastery now and experience the transformative power of Vastu Shastra.

Order Now and Receive:

- Immediate access to practical Vastu solutions.

- Tips and strategies to apply Vastu principles in modern living.

- A step-by-step guide to achieving balance and prosperity in all areas of life.

Limited Time Offer - Don't Miss Out!

Embrace the wisdom of Vastu Shastra and unlock the life you've always dreamed of. With our special "2 Books in 1" series, mastery is within your reach. Order your Vastu Bundle today and take the first step towards a brighter, more harmonious future!

Achieve Life Mastery with the Vastu Bundle!

Order Now and Transform Your Life!

1. Master Your DESTINY And CAREER With Vastu: 2 Books in 1

2. Master Your HOME HARMONY And WEALTH With Vastu: 2 Books in 1

3. Master Your HEALTH And RELATIONSHIPS With Vastu: 2 Books in 1

TESTIMONIALS

These are a few feedbacks from my clients across different parts of the world. Kindly go through their reviews to understand how numerology helped them.

1. Ekta Gupta – Kolkata, India

"2021 is a difficult year for me. I have consulted a few numerologists. I have received vague answers and complicated solutions. I'm new to numerology. Charges were expensive. Sooraj is a good and kind soul. He is very patient with me. He answered all my questions. I had 1000 questions. More ever he helped me to find a business name with no extra charges. I'm grateful to him. With your help, I'm sorted out with my business name. I had a lot of anxiety about it. I'm confident now. Sooraj is a helpful soul. He is patient and explains if one has questions. He doesn't rush into closing the job. You can consult him easily. I am going to recommend him to newbies like me. He is not going to cheat you or misguide you".

2. Neetu Ganglani - Stanley, Hongkong

"Hello Sooraj, I can't thank you enough. At the age of 45, I could find an ideal life partner for myself. And my compatibility with the boy I like. Got to know our strengths and weaknesses. Your suggestions helped me to find the right life partner. You have a bright future. Good luck"

3. R Lensly Kwaimani - Solomon Islands, Oceania

"Dear friend, glad I came across you. My daughter Felinda Kwaimani is sick for a long time and I was very much worried. Thank you for giving suggestions and guidance".

4. Seham Shabhir - Talagang, Pakistan

"You're one of the best numerologists...your predictions are correct...you are a very humble person...you gave answers to all of my questions in detail ... I'm very thankful to you. Ur remedies prove very helpful for me. He is the very best numerologist... I recommend him for all.. u should consult him to get rid of your problems..his remedies work like a magic"

5. Naveen Kumar - Bengaluru, India

"Sooraj is a gem as a human and as a professional. Before approaching Sooraj, I have enquired and got inputs from other numerologists and I did some research as well. I Was not satisfied with the answers provided by them and most of them were behind fees, even after paying for the consultation they charge extra for clarifying doubts. However, Sooraj was awesome in client satisfaction and the way he follows up with the client for providing suggestions. He takes the initiative to follow up and provide the best solutions and describes the reason for the input. I definitely suggest Sooraj to anyone who is looking for start-up business names or anything related to numerology. He has a good amount of knowledge and patience to answer all my queries".

6. Sneha S - Karnataka, India

"Hi Sooraj, it's a great prediction starting from Personality Traits to our Abroad Opportunities to future achievements. Everything is perfectly predicted with correct proof and explanations which help us to understand our lives better and take steps accordingly to numerology. Everyone are curious to know more about their life just to know when, how & what situations they will come across and how they need to overcome everything. Thanks a lot, Sooraj, for the best Numerology Prediction which helped us to understand ourselves better".

7. Aditya S - Mumbai, India

"Sooraj, your numerology predictions are brilliant and accurate. Your Suggestions helped me find out whether my current job is suitable for me or not. I would suggest people consult you in due course of time".

8. M Nabanita - West Bengal, India

"Hi Sooraj, it's helpful and gives me a quick idea and help. Thank you so much for being there. It helped me to understand my situation It helps in my career and marriage. The information is good".

9. Naresh Kumar – Bangalore, India

"Hello Sooraj, it was satisfactory. Can decide further based on the info shared & also can see positive outcomes looking forward to checking how it works".

10. Harishchandra Dnyaneshwar Deshmukh – Delhi, India

"Hi sir, Padhai puri nahi kar paya, 11 k salary he, Stable nahi hu life me, Business success nahi milta. Thank u sir for sharing my report and helping me understand my strengths and weaknesses".

AUTHOR PROFILE

 Follow **the Author's Profile Page** to get updates on all his books: **https://amazon.com/author/sooraj_achar**

 Grab your **Free Gift** if you missed it: **https://sooraj.soorajachar.com/free-gift**

Please Leave Your **Valuable Review** here: **"Master Your MONEY With Numerology"**

For 1-to-1 consultation, scan the **QR code** or contact: **infot@soorajachar.com**

Follow the **Author's BookBub** Profile:

https://www.bookbub.com/auth ors/sooraj-achar

Stay Connected to the **Author's Social Media Handles** below:

https://amzn.to/3CgQHF9

https://medium.com/@soorajachar99

https://bit.ly/3M7gIu2

instagram.com/psychology_of_numberz/

https://bit.ly/3dO6aDh

https://bit.ly/3LXBTyz

https://bit.ly/3E9vKxc

DISCLAIMER

This book is for educational purposes only. Readers acknowledge that the author does not render legal, financial, medical, or professional advice. The content within this book has been derived from various sources. Please consult a licensed professional before attempting any techniques outlined in this book.

By reading this document, the reader agrees that under no circumstances is the author responsible for any direct or indirect losses incurred as a result of the use of the information contained within this document, including but not limited to errors, omissions, or inaccuracies.

Adherence to all applicable laws and regulations, including international, federal, state, and local governing professional licensing, business practices, advertising, and all other jurisdictions, is the sole responsibility of the purchaser or reader.

Neither the author nor the publisher assumes any responsibility or liability whatsoever on behalf of the purchaser or reader of these materials. Any perceived slight of any individual or organization is purely unintentional.